SAILING INTO
Salvation

Ronald Barratt

ISBN 979-8-88832-937-5 (paperback)
ISBN 979-8-88832-938-2 (digital)

Christian Faith Publishing
832 Park Avenue
Meadville, PA 16335
www.christianfaithpublishing.com

Printed in the United States of America

ACKNOWLEDGMENTS

In approximately 2016, I approached my friend Mark Eberle, the founder of Paws Healing Heroes. I suggested that I may be able to help in his efforts to help veterans with PTSD, a crippling condition that many veterans face each day. In fact, it is estimated that up to twenty-two veterans take their own lives each day. Mark decided to intervene. He had been saving dogs from kill shelters, training them as service dogs, and then placing them with veterans fighting each day. After speaking with him, he suggested that I could use a dog myself. I scoffed at the idea, but as the conversation continued, I had to agree that I had a problem that a dog could help with. After a few years, I relented, and Shiloh came into my life. After only a week or so, I realized that Shiloh changed my life. She is alert and warns of danger, she calms me when anxiety hijacks my mind. She is a companion and a friend that I cannot imagine being without. This was the work of Paws Healing Heroes (pawshealingheroes.org). I cannot thank Mark enough. Shiloh has been a gift to me. In fact, after sharing so many stories with Mark, he suggested I write down my experiences. It was Mark's commitment and belief in me that what I had to say could influence veterans with PTSD and share the story of the Lord with anyone needing God's love. Some stories are funny, at least to us. I hope you enjoy them as well. Mark has shared his experience on the *Rachael Ray* show twice, and so far, he has helped seventy-five veterans with hope, encouragement, and a vision of the future through his efforts and those of the people around him. This is done entirely through donations. He has made an incredible impact on the lives of many veterans, including me. Thank you, Mark. It will take a lifetime for me to make it up to you. If you could find it in your heart to contribute to Mark's efforts, please visit pawshealingheroes.org. Somewhere out there, there are veterans, alone, in despair, and without hope. Together, we can all make a difference. Thank you, Mark!

GLASSBORO, NJ

I grew up in a small town in South Jersey called Glassboro. It was an incredible community and very diverse. My neighborhood and my experience in that neighborhood can only be characterized as a Norman Rockwell painting. We were very close as a neighborhood. Doors were never locked; a cup of sugar or a couple of eggs were always a door or two down.

Back before the Internet or video games, sports dominated our every waking moment. When I was eight years old, we had a Wiffle ball field on a farmer's field. Peach trees were everywhere as well as soybean, but we found an area that seemed to not be in use. One summer, when we were setting up the field to play, we had to mow since the brush had grown over two feet. All of us got our father's mowers and headed for the field. As we were mowing, a tractor turning over the soil to prepare for planting, we assumed, was heading for us. The tractor grew closer and closer; we knew this year we would not be playing Wiffle ball anymore. The farmer, a man called Rowand, evidently told his people to let us use his land. The tractor got very close to our field and simply turned and went around. Wow, we thought, *How lucky are we?* This is a simple story, but one that depicts a very close-knit community.

In mid-June of that year, I woke up with intense pain in my right side, which I could not explain. I told my mother, and she decided to keep a close eye on me from then on. Was it hunger pain? Maybe something related to digestion? After three or four days, she took me to our family physician for answers. The doctor, who everyone in the town saw, I think, gave me some basic tests. Vitals were taken. I'm not sure if blood was taken, but I can remember one test that should have told the entire story. He pushed on the right side of my stomach. There was no pain until he let go. The pain was intense. The doctor explained to my mother that the symptoms were mimicking appendicitis, an inflammation in my appendix. "Nothing to worry about. We've seen false appendicitis cases lately," he said, and off we went. The pain persisted over the next couple of weeks. I was really looking forward to the Fourth of July that year. Nothing excited me more than fireworks.

We went to our close friends' house who had a pool, and I remember being very angry with my mother because I could not swim. I remember feeling worse as each hour passed. I developed a high fever. My mother took me to the local hospital. Blood tests confirmed that my appendix had burst, and now we were dealing with peritonitis. My bowels had basically leaked into my stomach cavity, and my body was in overdrive in an attempt to attack the poison that led to a life-threatening situation. I was rushed to the operating room to remove my appendix.

After the surgery, as you can imagine I was incredibly sore. I was eight years old and really knew nothing more than sports, the Phillies and the Eagles. My temperature was very high but understandably so. The one thing I can remember were the needles, the constant needles. Even at eight, I could be brave and take the pain. I thought to myself, *Do this and don't make Mom or Dad see you in pain.* I found out that it is easy to be brave short-term. Long-term bravery in dealing with pain is a different beast. Now, looking back, it is profound typing these words, considering what was to come later in life.

My temperature continued to remain high in the coming days and weeks. We found out later that the doctor had removed my appendix but failed to clean out all the poison that had leaked into my body. As the weeks followed, my demeanor changed from cooperative to downright combative. I was sick of the pain; I was sick of being sick. The needles drove me crazy, and I counted every single one. If, in the morning, a nurse would come in to give me a needle, I would call my mother crying. She would jump out of bed and rush to the hospital. The nurses had been understanding and would wait for my mother to get there. One morning, a nurse came in as usual. Once again, I called my mother and asked the nurse to wait. She did for a while. After about fifteen minutes, she lost her patience and tried to administer the needle without Mom there. I began to fight her. She called in two other nurses to hold me down. I was brawling with three nurses as my mom walked in. Only then did I relent. It was a funny moment my mother later related to me. "When I saw that, I knew I had a fighter on my hands."

As time went on, my fever would not come down despite all the antibiotics they had pumped into my system. High fevers can be tolerated in young children longer than adults. This is what I was told years later anyway. In adults, high fevers are very dangerous and can cause brain damage and even death. The same is true for children, but they have time that adults do not have. I have no idea if this is true, but that is what I was told. My temperature was consistently over 106 degrees, and time was not on our side. After three weeks, the fever would not break. At this time, I remember no longer being able to concentrate as well as I had earlier. I could, however, sense that urgency was on the minds of my parents and the doctors. They were trying different antibiotics, but nothing seemed to work.

The doctor took my mother aside and asked her to sign a waiver. The waiver was for an antibiotic that was meant only for adults, or so I was told much later. The danger in this antibiotic, the doctor explained, was that it could damage me in other areas. The doctor mentioned that it could affect my ability to produce children later. That was not exactly a priority at the time. My mother signed. I remember my father being there and speaking confidently to me for quite a while. "Ah, this will work itself out, Ronnie, just hang in there." When the nurse came in, I believe he was new to the profession. As the needle went into my arm, he made some kind of mistake, and the needle bent to a ninety-degree angle. My father almost fainted. The nurse tried a second time and was successful. Now we had to wait.

After twenty-four hours, I could sense the urgency increasing. I really didn't think in terms of actual possible results. I had no idea what death was, really. All I knew was football season was right around the corner, and I was at the age where I could play organized football for the first time. *Get this over with!* That night, the doctors told my mother that they were going to have to operate a second time. This time, they were going to cut me from the top of my stomach down to my groin and clean out what was causing the infection that put my life in jeopardy. They were out of options, Mom was told. The problem was that I had lost twenty-five pounds already as a result of not being able to keep anything down that I ate. The odds were not good that I would survive another surgery. No choice, Mom was told. After three weeks of 106 temperatures, my brain was going to fry. They gave me an ice bath, something that they no longer do. I loved it. I was burning up for weeks and loved the relief. The ice melted away. I waited for surgery in the morning.

When I woke up, my mother was over me crying. I thought something was wrong or I upset her somehow. Wrong. My fever broke. My life was spared, I thought. God Almighty Himself saved me. I never said this out loud at the time, but I thought, and still do, that I was saved to do something impactful. Of course, at the time, I thought I was going to become the middle linebacker for the Philadelphia Eagles and become famous.

As long as I can remember, all I wanted to do was play football. When I was four or five years old, I would watch the NFL specials that were out there. Crunch time, meanest linebackers, and the undersized NFL stars. They all had an impact on me, and I really didn't know why. I would set up couch cushions and stack them up in our living room and time the "hits" along with Jack Lambert, Dick Butkus, or "Mad Dog" Mike Curtis. They were my heroes. I remember seeing a special on a cornerback called Pat Fischer from the Washington Redskins (Commanders). He was tiny and would launch himself into much larger opponents and put them on their butts. I loved his confidence and his willingness to share it on the field and off. Jack Lambert was an animal, and although he was tall, he was also undersized. He dominated the field physically and psychologically. Dick Butkus? Just pull up YouTube and you'll see the absolute destruction he caused for his opponents. Mike "Mad Dog" Curtis of the Baltimore Colts was another man I dreamed of being. I remember one quote from a teammate that made me laugh every time. "I've never seen a man unhappier on the day of a game in my life." Loved it. Why? I'm not sure. I was drawn to the battle between men, the battle of wills, and overcoming obstacles and pain. This would serve me well in the years ahead.

At this point, I thought it would be helpful to introduce you to my mother and father. My mother, Catharine is a tough, fiery character, quick to anger and even quicker to love. Our relationship was very contentious, but also very loving. My father, Bob, was a very special man. He grew up poor as many of the time did. His father was an alcoholic, and from what I'm told, my grandmother was as well. He was a natural athlete and leader and had an older brother and younger sister. My earliest memories of Dad were of him taking me everywhere he went. He coached baseball in the spring and football in the fall. Dad carried himself with a confidence that seemed out of place to many who didn't know him. But to those who did know him, that confidence was earned. He was incredibly inclusive. When he was a kid, everyone was welcomed to play on the fields they used regardless of race or age. Everyone loved him. More on Mom and Dad later.

In my hometown, it was expected to participate in sports, especially in my neighborhood. It's amazing how many great athletes came out of a small neighborhood like ours. One of my dear friends and neighbors went on to come third in the Heisman Trophy voting when he played at the College of the Holy Cross. Crazy.

Early on, football was very important to me. I couldn't start until I was nine years old because of my surgery, and I was very upset about it. But once I hit nine years old, I was off and running. At that age, I wasn't incredibly small for my age, and I did very well. In my town, I was one of maybe three or four white kids in the program. The entire program was run by my black American friends and coaches whom I admired. My coach, Dave Smith, would come from work as a mechanic right over to the field across the street. He was so encouraging and complimentary that I wanted desperately to excel because of him. I needed his acceptance. This would carry on for the rest of my life.

In high school, I played for John Aveni, a legend in my hometown. Coach Aveni had gone on the play in the NFL after playing college ball at Indiana University for the Washington Redskins. I idolized this man. My father, who was a quarterback in high school and a member of the hall of fame, also coached for years under John Aveni. As a youngster, I would always hang out in the coach's room before and after games. I knew to keep my mouth shut and be a fly on the wall. I learned what he and the other coaches wanted to see and expected. I learned which players they admired and others who were not in their good graces. I couldn't wait to play for them. I got my wish once I turned fifteen as a freshman.

In my sophomore year, I was assigned to play middle linebacker like I always dreamed of. The problem was that I didn't know how to approach the position. By now, I was completely undersized at five feet, seven inches and maybe 165 pounds. I now was among monsters. *What do I do?* I struggled so much in the beginning. I was completely confused and outsized. *Hmm. Let's figure this out.* I began to view the offense as a whole. I started to predict plays that were to be run and knew based on many factors where the ball was going. I figured it out. I thrived as a junior and especially in my senior year. I thought I *was* Jack Lambert. I looked at field position, down and distance, and formation of the offense. After looking at film all week, I realized that based on formation, there were possible plays and *probable* plays. With this information in hand, I became very successful. At the time, I thought I was the best linebacker in the world and deserved a scholarship to a major division one program. I had a lot to learn.

During my senior year, I was being honored at the local country club as "back of the week." There was a coach from some college there to give a pitch on how great his school was and why someone should pick Trenton State College (now The College of New Jersey). I was reluctant to speak to him since the year before, I was honored by the South Jersey Coaches Association (or something like that) as the back of the week as well. I believe it was The Brooks-Irvine Club, whatever that was. That year, I sat next to Andy Talley, head coach at Villanova University. I was nervous and wanted to strike up a conversation and mentioned maybe playing for him. Now, keep in mind this guy is the same size as me, short. He looked me up and down and said, "Go try a Division III school." Boy, was I insulted! Not that I thought I would actually play for him, but to insult a young kid who was at an event celebrating his success was rude. I was angry. The next year, I sat next to Eric Hamilton of Trenton State College. From my experience the year before, I didn't want to open myself up to another awkward situation. My dad walked up and said, "Coach, this is my son Ronnie. Why don't you exchange information?" We did.

By this time, I realized that my size was a problem to overcome. I just wanted a chance somewhere. I visited Glassboro State College (now Rowan University) in my hometown. I knew the coach well, and my high school coaches did too. They gave me the thumbs-up to him. As I sat there, I got the usual questions: How tall are you? How much do you weigh? What is your forty time? Blah blah blah. I found myself burning with anger. I reminded him that I played about three hundred yards from where we were sitting. Never bothered to see a game? Very forward and inappropriate. Keep in mind that I had "little guy syndrome." I found any question of my ability insensitive and insulting. *If you think I can't play, put a helmet on and see for yourself.* I decided to visit Trenton State College.

My best friend, Frank Mancini, and I went for a visit. Frank was an amazing all-around athlete, and I was a bit nervous that Coach Hamilton would have no interest in me. I was wrong. We gave our "audition" tapes to Coach Ham, and off we went. After touring the school and speaking to players who were already there, we returned to the athletic building where the coaches offices were. Coach Hamilton walked out with a big smile on his face with his hand extended. He simply said, "You can play for me any time. Whether you start or not is up to you." I instantly said yes. I finally had an opportunity to prove what no one else thought I could do.

My freshman year was a complete wake-up call. I was among other athletes just like me. Division III athletes don't get scholarships; we play for the love of the game. In many of the players, there is massive ability but with just one thing missing. Maybe a guy is great but can't run. Others lack good hands, a strong arm, something that drove them to a Division III program. Well, I was getting my lunch handed to me. My first experience with live contact came against an offensive guard who was very short and looked like a fire hydrant. It was set up as two linemen and two linebackers with a running back to follow. Our job was to defeat the blocker and tackle the running back. I got put on my back. I remember thinking to myself, *I better pick it up.* I should have known better than to judge a book by its cover. After that play, I hit as hard as I could and began to see success. I started at inside linebacker as a junior and really had to use my head to be successful since I was so small compared to my competition. I was five feet, eight inches with spikes on and two hundred pounds. Opposing linemen were 260 pounds and above. Running backs and fullbacks dwarfed me. I had a chip on my shoulder.

Where was God in all of this? I grew up Catholic, so I had God covered. I don't know if I just didn't pay attention or it just wasn't important to me at the time, but I thought, *I believe in God, Jesus, and the Holy Spirit. I'm a good guy, I think. I got it.* It would be years before I was drawn to God's love. At the time, I had football as my first and only priority. I remember the hardest game I ever played was in 1989 against Montclair University. They were our hated rivals that always seemed to have our number. Montclair was, and still is, a very successful program. That year, their offense was truly menacing. Their offensive line averaged 280 pounds, and they ran like receivers. Their fullback was 225 pounds and tough as nails, and their running back was getting NFL attention. I didn't sleep the night before.

By game time, it was eighty degrees and sunny. Great weather for people in the stands but burning hot on our artificial turf. I played that day as hard as I possibly could and was physically battered. I remember them running the same play directed at me individually many times during the course of the game; it is called isolation (target one man). The fullback would lead the play at me and try to blast a hole in our defense over *me.* I was insulted that they thought I was a weak link on the defense. I took it personally. I remember thinking, *Okay, let's see how this goes. You want to run me over? You're going to have to earn it.* Every time they ran this play, I joined the fullback in a ridiculous collision. Time and again, play after play, *bang!* I had no interest in where the runner was; I knew I had ten other guys on the field with me. They could take down the runner. I continually "restricted the running lane," meaning if I clog the hole in the backfield, the runner has nowhere to go. We ended up tying that day, and I walked away with the worst concussion I ever had. My memory of the day is cloudy; the sky looked green to me. I had blackouts during the game. I refused to give in to these bullies on my field. I was willing to do anything for them to never make the mistake of underestimating me again. I played this way every game. I took this mentality off the field, getting in fights and getting in trouble.

My coaches and teammates accepted me; they believed in me. I won their respect. To this day and for the end of my days, I will regard Coach Hamilton and Kelly Myers (defensive coordinator) as friends and mentors whom I love.

My senior year came to an end. We were more successful as a football team than any team up to that point. I played baseball and was a catcher on the team that went to the college world series. I needed to graduate at this point. I was scared. *What do I do then? Where do I go?* The future was uncertain. In the fall of 1992, I decided to join the United States Navy.

UNITED STATES NAVY

In the summer of 1992, I had my eye on becoming a New Jersey State Trooper. I had studied criminal justice for that purpose. At this point, I had learned that the state had put on hold any hiring of new trainees and that now they required a college degree or four years on the military. I was delivering pizza and bartending for a college bar that was now empty because of students going home for summer vacation. Going home was out of the question. I had no interest in living under my parents' roof anymore primarily because I knew my mother would make it challenging. Over the course of my college experience, I had been told repeatedly that I was "nothing more than a financial burden." I was reminded constantly about the financial sacrifices my mother had made. I had done what I could to lessen that burden; I worked every summer and handed over my checks and coached football once my playing days were over and handed those checks over as well. There wasn't much more I could do, so I put my head down, graduated, and decided to never go back.

Since the state police had stopped their hiring, I was in a bind. Delivering pizza and bartending were not paying the bills, and I fell behind putting pressure on my friends and roommates. I was driving through Ewing, New Jersey, and saw a navy recruitment center. I had a brilliant idea, or at least I thought it was. *What if I join the military? That way I will meet both of the state's criteria for hiring in the state police.* I stopped by the recruiting station the next day. What would I like to do in the navy? Of course, like many young guys with nothing but testosterone pumping through their veins, I wanted to be a Navy SEAL. I knew what it was like to push myself beyond any limitations I thought I had. I was young, in shape, and overconfident. I mentioned the idea to the recruiter, Jim Orcut, a fat, sloppy guy who was an aircraft technician of some sort. I asked about becoming an officer.

He said, "Oh no, we don't do that anymore."

Not only was that a ridiculous response, but how dumb was I to fall for it? I had no idea that there was a difference between an enlisted recruiter and an officer recruiter. I had my eyes on being a SEAL anyway, so who cared?

I remember the height and weight requirements. I thought to myself, *Really? Size again?* I had dealt with reporters since I was sixteen years old. There were headlines such as "Barratt Plays No Small Role" or "There's LITTLE Barratt Can't Do." Not very creative. More insulting than anything else. I was All-South Jersey Group 1 first team and All-South Jersey All-Groups third team. Maybe it was possible I could play the game a little bit? Was it a fluke that I set the record for career tackles at my high school that still stands in 2022? Getting myself a bit worked up here. The point is I had a chip on my shoulder, and here comes the navy at me about size. Their point of view was a bit different, though. I was five feet, eight inches and weighed 193 pounds at the time. To me this was perfectly normal. I was stocky and strong. I was required to come in at 178 pounds because of my vertically challenged body. Oh boy. I went home and began working out constantly. I ran four miles twice a day. I ran bleachers at Glassboro State College, which is now Rowan University. I worked out with weights, but most importantly, I began vastly limiting my food intake to lose weight. I wasn't given a SEAL guarantee, meaning it would be uncertain if I would be accepted into BUD/S, Basic Underwater Demolition/SEAL. I had to report to my first command and work my way into getting permission for training.

I was granted admission into the intelligence field of the navy called intelligence specialist. I liked the idea of working in intelligence, although at the time I had no idea what that would entail. I knew that I had to go to boot camp and then on to intelligence training in Virginia. My focus, however, was to be a badass SEAL. Had no idea what I was getting myself into. I could swim, run, do push-ups all day, and had a nasty, never-give-up mentality that would serve me well later on in life, but all I wanted was to serve my country on the front lines. In retrospect, there were plenty of other options to do just that, but I had blinders on and wanted what I wanted. The *one* thing I didn't take into consideration: Could I stand the cold? Found out later that BUD/S candidates are basically tortured with cold, being sandy almost constantly, and basically being miserable almost all the time. Again, being miserable and dealing with it would come much later, but I definitely had to give this a second thought. *Ah, I'll worry about that later. Just give me an opportunity and I'll find a way to make it work.* Yeah, okay, keep telling yourself that, big guy.

I got a call from my recruiter about two weeks later after signing my name. Jim told me that they had a boot camp spot open, and it was mine if I wanted it. When, I asked. Two weeks. Two weeks? I had to lose sixteen pounds in *two* weeks. I accepted and began starving myself while also working out like a madman. I ran and ran again. I also enlisted my brother, Bryan, and my wrestling coach in high school, Steve Cifonelli, to wrestle with me. I definitely had my hands full then! My brother was a national champion at 150 pounds at Glassboro State College, and Steve was a nationally ranked wrestler at Temple University. They took turns pounding on me as the pounds came off slowly. I literally had nothing left. Not one drop of fluid was left in me, and I was as sucked down in weight I could be. I had to make weight the following day in Philadelphia.

I had never been so desiccated or dehydrated in my life. I was exhausted and just wanted to get the weigh-in done so I could qualify to apply for BUD/S in the future. I waited for over an hour with the anticipation of drinking four Gatorades in a row once I was done. Finally, my name was called. At weigh-in, they took my weight, 176 pounds. Yes! I made weight. The gentleman taking my weight hesitated, and I had no idea why. He got on the phone. I could hear him say, "Sir, Ronald Barratt made the required weight, but he shrank an inch. He's five-seven." *What? Oh boy, now what? I can't lose another ounce.* He got off the phone and told me they would give me a pass. Whew. And yes, I did drink four Gatorades in a row. I was off to Great Lakes, Illinois, for boot camp.

*****

The trip was scary. I had not been in an uncomfortable position since not knowing what to expect my freshman year at Trenton State College. When we got to boot camp, we were in a large hangar with what seemed like thousands of other kids. We were shuffled here and there when someone asked if anyone would be interested in either the band, drill team, or the choir. I raised my hand since I had been singing my whole life. We were taken to a large room above the hangar where we met a chief petty officer who ran the choir. He sat at a piano with two hundred new sailors standing in line. He would tap two keys on the piano, and one at a time, we were asked to mimic that key with our voices. I remember the kid in front of me was awful, break-glass awful, and I felt bad for him. When it was my turn, he played the first two keys, and I imitated the sound I heard with "la la." He then played two more, two more to determine my range, I guess. He then had me sing happy birthday in the key of his choosing. I did, and he simply replied, "Nice." I was in the choir. Those chosen for the choir were whisked to a boot camp company comprised of choir members, drill team, and band members. Our company commander was waiting.

In boot camp, half of the class had already been a week ahead of us, and I had no idea that, that would become an issue until later. Our company commander (drill sergeant) was a guy called Eric Harriman. He was short, wide, and very loud. Exactly what I expected. I had never heard a man yell louder than ET1 Harriman (Electronics Technician First-Class). This was going to be the longest two and a half months of my life. The first two weeks in boot camp, we were taught how to fold our uniforms and make beds and were taken to classes to learn the basics of the United States Navy. After two weeks, I couldn't have cared less. Yelling stopped bothering me, and I could do push-ups all day if they wanted me to. I do remember being disappointed that, although we worked out, we hardly ever got out for a run since it was minus ten degrees in Great Lakes during winter. We did work out inside the barracks, and they had a fascination with "Super Ricks." This was when a recruit (Rick) would lie flat on his stomach and put his hands out in front of him (Superman-like) with our backs arched. He would then torture us with staying in the same uncomfortable position for as long as the navy would allow. I also remember the weakness I saw in my fellow recruits. Out of shape, overweight, sloppy kids who thought joining the navy meant nothing more than pushing buttons or something. *They're problem*, I thought. There was one thing that was enlightening and disappointing to me about the navy. Toward the end of boot camp, we were required to wear a white belt over our navy-issued jackets. One day in the chow hall, a young sailor out of boot camp maybe a week made fun that I was still not graduated. He looked down, noticed my belt, and made a snide remark. I was furious and asked ET1 Harriman if this was something I would have to get used to. I told him I didn't think I could swallow my pride much longer. He just gave me a concerned look. I would find out later that rank is what everyone sees first, and people make spot judgments based on the number of stripes you have. I was off to intelligence training.

After two weeks off and visiting my family and friends from Glassboro, I headed to Dam Neck, Virginia, a few miles from Virginia Beach for intelligence training. I was housed near the Navy and Marine Corps Intelligence Training Center (NMITC). At this point, my expectations were high, and I thought I would finally be in a position to concentrate solely on becoming an intelligence specialist. I had no idea that there would be a lack of teamwork or teammate atmosphere. I was disappointed. School started off during March of 1993. My recollection of events at training school is a bit sketchy, but I did meet one of my friends whom I have to this day, twenty-nine years later, Jim Baker. I began calling him Meat back then after a character from the movie *The Wanderers*. It stuck.

Classes were progressing, but I found myself frustrated. I was having a hard time learning strictly from books. I would find out years later that I learn much better audibly and began reading out loud to learn. There were a few weeks dedicated to giving briefings or oral presentations about a specific military subject. I was tasked with doing a briefing on North Korea's leader, Kim Il Sung. I had to put together slides on an overhead projector, outlining his full biography and leadership of North Korea. Amazing how long ago that was; computers hadn't hit the navy yet, I imagine. Anyway, I did very well since I never had difficulty with public speaking. I was still struggling with the book-learning part, however. Our instructors were leadership challenged. They had an air of entitlement and arrogance and showed absolute contempt for their junior sailors sitting in their classes. In fact, many were not junior, just changing ratings (specialty). They had contempt for them too. Because of the graduating class's written reviews, they were all given warnings by the program's top commander. Accountability! As a result of struggling with the material, I was given an academic review board headed by an old salty chief petty officer. I promised to do better, but I didn't. I was held back two weeks to repeat the final stage all over again. I *knew* word would get back to my first command, whatever that was going to be. My name was muddied before I even started.

I got through the academic part by sheer providence and went on to real intelligence work in analysis. This would be accompanied with a briefing. Finally, something I can do well. We were broken down into groups with one trainee assigned to aircraft intelligence, naval, and radar intelligence. We were each given a packet with the information we were to chart on a map and use during our briefing. I got my intel packet and took note of all the relevant information. I then looked through all the other packets, not knowing if this was right or not. I got a mental picture of enemy A planning an attack at a bottleneck portion of ocean B. When I briefed, I included everything, not just the information I had been given. The reaction of the old salty chief that thought I was going to be a total failure was worth the wait. "Barratt just blew me out of the water!" I heard him utter down the hall. I'm not sure if he intended for that pun, but I was happy I finally did something right.

During the final month I was in Dam Neck, I called Marcy and asked her to marry me again. Her father had scared me so much in our first sit-down meeting that I called off any marriage plans. Now, wherever I was going, I wanted her with me. This was exacerbated by prayer since I had no idea what to do. I prayed, "Lord, guide me in the right direction" as we were marching to our classes, and an idea popped into my head. I knew it was the right thing to do. I should have known then and there that the Lord intervenes when you need

Him and ask Him. I had such a feeling of relief in what I needed to do that I should have dropped to my knees then and there and thank the Lord for His guidance. It took me far too long to realize that there are no coincidences; it's just the Lord's will. Missed that one until much later, but when we got to school, I called. "Wherever I go, I want you with me."

She said, "You know what that means?"

I said I did. I drove home from Virginia and got married on June 12, 1993. When I got back to Virginia, I had to wrap things up and find out where I would be stationed. They allow sailors to put in requests, but as a newbie, I didn't get my hopes up. I asked for east coast shore duty. I got west coast sea duty. Ha! I'll bet the sailor in charge of filling billets must have laughed pretty hard at my request. I was headed to the USS *Abraham Lincoln* (CVN-72), which had deployed already and was on the way to the Persian Gulf.

The USS *A. Lincoln* was based out of Naval Air Station Alameda, in California. Alameda is a neighbor of Oakland and across the bay from San Francisco. There was nothing incredible to report about my check-in, but once again, I was clueless of where to go, who to report to, and so on. I was given a "dorm room" of sorts, on my own. President Clinton had decided to close many bases at the time, and Alameda was on the chopping block. As a result, the place was becoming more and more of a ghost town as the days went on. I assume this was the reason I was given my own room in the barracks. The facilities were fine, very nice actually, and there were others on my floor. I finally found out where to go and began the waiting process. The navy wasn't just going to fly one or two guys out to the ship; they wanted to wait until the plane could be close to being filled. Made sense. In the meantime, I was tasked, along with others, to work on the base while we waited. I checked in with several other guys, and we were given jobs like picking up trash on the base, painting, and other "keep busy" things to do. We stayed busy for two weeks waiting for a plane.

The base was very nice, I thought. They had a PX, which I have no idea what that stands for, but it was a store for navy members on the base to shop. There were things like uniforms, a tailor shop, and many other things that resembled a mini-Walmart. At this point, I was incredibly lonely but thought that must be normal. I tried to stay busy, especially at night. They had a bar that seemed to be filled almost nightly. Sailors drink? I had no idea! Joking, of course. I was always an outgoing guy, so I did what I could to speak to other folks who were there to combat the loneliness. I also realized how naive I actually was. I thought sharing the uniform meant that we were all brothers, part of a team. I guess, looking back, I should have known that the navy is the biggest military force we have, something like four hundred thousand sailors at the time or something. There were bound to be some knuckleheads mixed in along with other people. There were drug dealers around, which I was not interested in. I thought, *If that is what you want to do, why join the navy? You can be a drug dealer anywhere.* Bringing it on base was stupid and reckless. I also found out there were others there stalking their prey. I was speaking to a young lady one night, just chitchat. It was country music night. Country music was something that I had never been introduced to but over time learned to appreciate. The other thing I really liked about country music night were the ladies who seemed to have some kind of need to wear extremely tight jeans. Yeah, I know, I was married, but there was some kind of force that I had no control over that lead me to enjoy the scenery. This young lady was married, I believe, and she seemed genuinely interested in who I was, where I came from, and so on. It never occurred to me that she was working an angle. Her husband was out to sea, and she was left alone on base until he returned. There was line dancing going on, something that was so foreign to me it made me a bit squeamish. What were they doing? I was dumbfounded. She insisted on teaching me. My face turned white, and my heart raced knowing I would fall or something. She tried to show me for about two minutes before my embarrassment was too much for me to handle. That was when she decided to appeal to my loneliness and gullible stupidity. She asked if I was looking to maybe chat with her in private, maybe back at her place. Now, picture a completely inexperienced guy who has never seen the real world and thinks that people are generally kind. I was very uncomfortable with the "back at my place" suggestion, and I mustered up about a grain of sand's worth of common sense.

"I'm not sure what you mean, but I really don't think it is a good idea going back to your place. Why can't we just talk here?" Good, right?

She replied, "For $200 I can show you why."

Okay, uh-huh. You would think at this point I would get it, right? I wish I could tell you that yes, I got it, and ran in terror. Nope, I had to hear it from her, and I had the gall to actually ask the following, "You're a prostitute?" *Dude, seriously?* Did I really just ask that? *No kidding, you idiot! Run!*

Okay, first lesson learned. The next day, I got done picking up trash or whatever we had to do that day and returned to the barracks. There really wasn't much to do, no cell phones, no computers, not even a newspaper that I could find. I'm not sure what exactly I was doing when a marine knocked on my semi-opened door and came in. He was a staff sergeant, which means he was three pay grades ahead of me. He was an E-6, the E representing the enlisted ranks. I was a seaman, or an E-3. In the military, it may take someone eight to ten years to become an E-6, so I was a bit intimidated, and I certainly was not used to someone of that high of a rank wanting to talk to me. I accepted it, though; it was nice to speak to anyone really. He was about five feet ten and 160 pounds with the military issue eyeglasses, very 50s look. We spoke for a while, and he left. *What a nice guy*, I thought. Our plane was going to be here in the next day or two; now my nerves were off the rails.

The night before I was set to leave the base and fly off to the Middle East, I was so nervous I couldn't breathe. I went down to the USO on base and had three beers, hoping it would allow me to sleep. I went up to my room, shut the door, and tried to sleep without success. I set the only alarm I had, which was my wristwatch. I remember looking at it: 3:00 a.m. Jeez, I was only going to be able to sleep three hours before I had to run off to the building near the tarmac. I'm sure you're already guessing what happened, right? Yep, I woke up and looked at my watch; it was 9:30 am! I missed my flight! Oh man, I cannot even begin to tell you the panic I felt knowing that in only six months of being in the navy, I had *two* major screwups now in the course of about three months. I had to repeat in intelligence school, and now I missed my stinking plane to get to my command! You have to give it to me; go big or go home. When I foul up, it's a doozy.

I ran to the building where I was supposed to report to. I can't remember the name of it, though. I found the nearest chief petty officer and "threw myself at the mercy of the court." I apologized profusely and took full responsibility for my stupid actions. He didn't rip me apart or anything; in fact, he was incredibly gracious about it, so much so that he reminded me of someone so chilled out they just smoked pot or something. He simply said that another plane was coming in a week. I remember thinking how kind this man was. In truth, what did he care? I wasn't one of his guys; I was not his responsibility. Either way, I appreciated it, but thinking of the obvious repercussions waiting, *that* was killing me. Word was on the way to the leadership of the USS *Abraham Lincoln* that Barratt made yet another boneheaded mistake. Yes, I was going to be regarded as a complete dunce and an incompetent buffoon. Gee, couldn't wait to see the looks on the faces of these guys that I didn't know yet. How stupid could I possibly be?

Before I go on, let me share with you the importance of chief petty officers in the navy. The enlisted, as well as the officer corps, are ranked from E-1 through E-9. In the case of officers, it goes O-1 through O-9. I was an E-3 as stated earlier, which I was given simply because I was a college graduate. A chief petty officer is an E-7, and throughout any branch of military force, they are considered vital. In fact, chiefs are commonly referred to as the guys who run the navy. Yes, even the officers would agree with that. Chiefs are the conduit between the enlisted and the officers. They are so important because they link the enlisted with the officers; without them, the officers would have no idea what was going on in the lower ranks. I would later meet a man who had just been promoted to chief petty officer who would make a major impact on my time in the navy and on my life. More about him later.

During the following week, I was torturing myself with guilt and worry. *How can I make up for this? I can't, really. The only thing I can do is press forward, chalk it up to a learning opportunity.* Yeah, right, I was scared to death. In reflection, I tend to let negative mistakes dominate my thoughts way too much. This is something I am still working on, and with the Lord in my heart, this has diminished considerably.

The night before I was set to fly out to the ship, I was on edge as you can expect. I left my door open about eight inches so I could have the light shine in my room. The thought was if I could ensure that the room was not pitch-black the entire time, I wouldn't miss my flight this time. I really never considered that this would set me up for a predator to enter my room. Unfortunately, that is exactly what happened.

I had been fighting sleep all night; I could *not* afford to miss my flight again. Of course, I fell asleep very late. I heard shuffling in my room. *Am I dreaming this, or do I open my eyes and see for myself?* With the minimal light that was coming into my room, I could see the staff sergeant rummaging in my packed bag. I was still half asleep and wasn't sure if I was actually seeing what I was seeing, and I could only see a silhouette, but it was him. I think I moaned "hey" or something, and he realized I was awake. He walked toward me with no hesitation. He began trying to talk his way out of it. At this point, it was evident he was drunk, slurring his words. I felt threatened, obviously, and wanted to get out of my rack to stop him from whatever he had on his mind. I wanted to get into a position where I could defend myself, get my legs under me, and out of a helpless position that the rack put me in.

Remember, I was naive and idealistic. We were teammates and we both loved our country. I was confused by what he was saying; at that point, it didn't matter to me. Maybe he was blackout drunk and didn't realize he was in the wrong room or something. He was going on that we got along so well during the week, and he felt comfortable with me. What was this guy talking about? Remember, the room was still dark, and he was babbling on about how much we got along and *how much he liked me.* I was stunned and totally panicking at this point. *What do I say to this man of much higher rank?* I thanked him for his interest and asked if I could walk him out of my room.

As we got up and headed toward the door, he asked if I would report this since he was a lifelong marine, or so I thought. I gave him a nervous answer that no, I had no interest or intention of ruining a man's career. Now his demeanor completely changed, his voice became deeper and more aggressive as well as feminine at the same time. His words became graphic. Okay, now I was completely at a loss on what to do. I grabbed his arm lightly above his elbow with the intention of helping him out of the room. Right near the door, he swung his arm free and hit me in the ribs very hard. I lost my breath briefly and began searching for him with my hands. I had been a wrestler in high school and figured I could keep him from injuring me if I could just get ahold of his hands. The struggle went on for what seemed like a lifetime. He continued hitting me and grabbing for my private area. Now I *really* needed to find his hands. I was only in skivvies at the time with a tee shirt on. I'd never felt so vulnerable in my life. He got a shot at my privates; I was instantly disabled and just couldn't reach my groin to protect myself. This may sound absolutely bizarre, but in my mind, I was thinking about my options. I had been in dozens of fights in my life up to that point and didn't think I lost one. I usually had little man syndrome and would act out aggressively even if it was inappropriate. Here I was, under attack and debating with myself if I should fight back! Can you believe this! I visualized destroying this guy physically, punching him over and over until the rage left me. The other side of the debate thought he was three pay grades ahead of me and people had seen the both of us talking in my room throughout the week. This would easily become my word versus his. Not one person in the navy would believe me; he's a higher rank. At the time, I also remember thinking, *My reputation is already in the toilet. This would not help that at all. What am I going to do? Stop everything, beat this guy to a pulp, and then report to my chain of command that he attacked me? Yeah, I don't think so.* Also, at the time, military sexual assault was swept under the rug; no one wanted this kind of thing getting out for public consumption. If you're thinking, "You thought all of this?" Yes, I did. I also thought that if I reported this, I would only ruin my own time in the navy. I would be hung up at this base for months probably, waiting for some investigation to go down, and so forth. I decided to get control of this guy, not hurt him in any recognizable way, and escort him out of my room, locking myself in until I had to leave.

Okay, where are his hands? Remember, it was very dark in my room then. When he hit me originally, he hit the light and shut the door. I was in searing pain because of his attack on my groin and now searching for his hands. I left my private area unguarded for approximately three seconds. Huge mistake. He found my penis and put it in his mouth. *How on earth did I get here? What do I do now?* He offered his teeth as a threat and a reminder that he was in complete control. To my everlasting shame that kills me to this day, my body behaved in a way that it would if I were with my wife. I can remember thinking I was in a dream world; this couldn't be happening to me. Thoughts of weakness and embarrassment and the real and persistent feeling of wanting to run as fast as I could away from this place. He got up, made a snide remark about how much more powerful he was, and slipped out of my room, never to be seen or heard from again.

I didn't chase him; I was too stunned and not sure exactly what I should do or how to react. I ran for the shower, dressed, made sure my bag was packed correctly, and waited for time to report. I got on the plane determined to reset my whole life. I needed to forget about this, first of all. Then I was determined to convince my chain of command on the USS *Abraham Lincoln* that I was competent and capable. I had to look forward and shake off the shame and embarrassment that just happened an hour ago.

The flight took off and headed to Philadelphia International. I met Mom and Dad there, still in a daze as a result of what happened eight hours earlier. We visited for a time and off to my next flight to Naples, Italy. That might have been the longest flight I could remember, and one I'd rather not repeat. I did, however, meet an amazing guy from Long Island, Chris Bottcher.

Bottcher was four years younger and bright-eyed and bushy-tailed, completely full of excitement. Man, I hated him for that. I wished I could join him. But, in the end, I admired him for wanting to serve this incredible country at eighteen years old. I only chatted briefly with him on the flight, if I can remember correctly, but we spoke again in Italy. We landed and got off the plane, not with a Jetway or whatever they call those things. We walked downstairs right off the plane onto the tarmac in crushing heat of summer. We ended up in some dank, run-down building with no air-conditioning. Wonderful. I don't think I could have been grumpier if you paid me to do it. There was a TV on and at least cold water available. Chris was standing in front of me blocking everything—view of the TV and the doorway in front of him.

"Dude, do you really think I can see through you? You're not a window, you know."

To his credit, he politely moved at my rude request and giggled to himself. After making it to the Middle East, Dubai in the United Arab Emirates, I believe, and a long bus ride, there it was, the USS *Abraham Lincoln* (CVN-72). *Incredible*, I thought. I couldn't believe something could be that big. And how did they make it float? I was awestruck.

They checked us in while most of the ship's crew were on liberty. We were taken to the ship's store to buy supplies such as soap, toothbrushes, toothpaste, towels, and things of that nature. We were standing in line to pay for our items, and there he was again, Chris Bottcher. He looked at the items in my little carry basket. He noticed that I had a lock and key among other things.

"Oh, hey, man, can you grab me one of those?" God love this guy; he'd been a thorn in my side since we left, and I had been moody and rude.

"Sure, man, anything else I can get for you? Need me to rub your feet? Shine your shoes? Anything, man, I am here for *you*."

We laugh about it now, but that was the anger I carried since my encounter back at NAS Alameda. It would continue for years.

CARRIER INTELLIGENCE CENTER (CVIC)

As discussed in the latter part of the previous chapter, I mentioned that I was now walking around with anger, frustration, and an overall poor disposition. I did not think of my visitor back in Alameda; to me that was gone, never to be thought of or spoken of ever again. Just as a spoiler, I didn't speak of it until twenty-five years later. I had a job to do and a division of peers that I had to convince I was a capable sailor. We had a week of indoctrination in a space on the ship toward the bow and just under the flight deck. It was basic teaching of how the ship is laid out, how to find our way around, and what to avoid. Me and Bottcher sat together and became fast friends; we laughed over and over about my smart-ass remarks, and he shared that since he was from New York, he appreciated my disagreeable attitude. "Thanks," I said with a laugh. We paid attention but passed the time naming an actor and then taking turns listing movies they were in. It was a fun exercise. He was a helmsman, who would later drive the ship and park it in port; incredibly impressive if you ask me. I can't back my car into a parking space, and this guy was parking a 1,200-foot ship with precision.

I checked in to the intelligence center called CVIC. CV stands for carrier, and IC is intelligence center. I was assigned to the administration office, which is a tiny space, enough room for maybe three men. Connected to that is the intel center's office for the commander. Our leader was a full-blown commander called CDR Cobery. He was a real treat to be around. He was constantly miserable and had no interest in the intel center, what we did, or how. He was a former helicopter pilot just finishing out his twenty years. He spent his time yelling and playing solitaire. He also had naked pictures of his wife hanging around his office! Yes, he did. Completely inappropriate and creepy. Why would anyone *want* to have pictures of their wife naked for all to see? His wife was from China, I believe, and he spoke Mandarin. This guy was flat-out weird. Remember, I was nothing, just a guy right out of boot camp, completely blown away any time I saw his silver leaf on his collar, and he blew any of my perceptions of qualified officers with yelling and screaming, playing solitaire, and looking at pictures of his naked wife. *What do I do if I have to go into his office? Look? Don't look? Dude freaks at the drop of a hat. What will he do if I look at these ridiculous pictures?* I chose to divert my eyes, keep my head down, and avoid this creep at all costs.

The lieutenant commander was some strange guy who was a reservist whom I didn't give a second thought to. *Reservist, yuck. What is he doing here? Go play on weekends somewhere, will you?* I know it sounds harsh, and it is. He was serving like the rest of us, but for some reason, we all had reservations about reservists, pun intended. He would inject himself on occasion, only to be a nuisance, like cleaning inspections. His name is Robert something, who cares?

I was introduced to my leading petty officer (LPO), Randy Brown. He was a first class petty officer with an air warfare rating; he had his enlisted wings. We became friends after a while, but at first, this guy had nothing but contempt for me since my reputation had already checked on board before I did. On a carrier or any other ship, supplies are needed to keep things going smoothly. We never had to fuel the ship or anything since it was nuclear-powered, but we did need food from time to time. Bringing food on board was done by lower-ranked sailors standing shoulder to shoulder, passing boxes off to the next guy. This exercise was called a working party. Yeah, party, huh? Right. Randy was aggressive with me from the beginning and would get a call about a working party every once in a while. He would hang up the phone and say something like, "Hey, Barratt, you're going to want to get your sorry ass down to the hangar bay for a working party. Got a problem with that?" Yeah, very professional. I never understood why in the military some leaders would resort to these kinds of exchanges. We were in the military; there was a chain of command. Orders were given to junior sailors, and we had to follow them regardless of how the orders were delivered. So why would you want to be degrading while giving them? Well, he thought very little of me and enjoyed humiliating me for some reason. He loved that power; that is the only thing I can think of. I wish I could tell you that I took it well. My visitor back in Alameda had made it very clear that he had complete power over me and enjoyed the humiliation he inflicted. I would get very angry when Randy would exert his power over me. I would follow orders, of course, but he could tell it bothered me, and he enjoyed that. After weeks and weeks of being the only person in the division to be sent for working parties, I decided to beat Randy to the punch. When he would get a call for someone from our division, I would volunteer. "I'll go, send me, would love to help." Shockingly, this took the air out of his balloon and stopped sending me. He would randomly pick junior guys to go. Problem solved.

Our chief petty officer select was Fred Hyde. He was still an E-6 but was in the process of transitioning to khakis. He would prove to be an incredible leader and teacher for me, but more about him later. At this point, I had been on board for maybe three weeks, and I realized that sleeping was becoming a problem. Our sleeping quarters, or birthing, was a room with twenty-two men in the same space. Our bunks, or racks, were stacked three high, and I was in the bottom rack. I remember a strange feeling in my chest when I would try to fall asleep. It was annoying, and I had no idea what it really was. It was accompanied by flop sweating, and I was very uncomfortable. I would relieve this condition by hanging my head out of my rack and would fall asleep. Then the real problems came with nightmares and night terrors.

At this point, I had some less-than-friendly leaders. I didn't mind too much; my intent was to win everyone over if given the chance to prove I could be a contributor to the overall mission. At the time, however, I had two second-class petty officers who enjoyed making me miserable, Ray Kemp and Mark Prince. They had both been in the navy for over four years, and I think they thought it was their responsibility to ride me into submission. That was difficult for me, and I disagreed with this kind of "leadership." Maybe they were asked to do this by the chain of command. I'm not sure; I never asked them. Kemp would go on to become master chief petty officer of the entire navy, a wildly impressive accomplishment, and we became close while he was there on board with me. I never got to know Prince all that well, but all is in the past. At the time, however, I just needed a chance to prove myself.

One of our duties was to man the desk watch. That was a desk sitting behind a window so we could see who was trying to come into the intel center. Since our spaces were for top-secret cleared personnel, we had to make sure we knew who was coming in. We would buzz those cleared and stop those who were not. One day I was on desk watch when I finally asked Randy Brown what the wings represented. I assumed it had to do with aircraft but wasn't sure. He told me about the program and even showed me the Bernoulli effect on aircraft. Apparently, this guy came up with the principle of fixed-wing flight; the shape of the wing induces lift. Randy took a piece of paper, held it on both edges, and let the paper sag while holding it. He mentioned that if he blew over the top of the paper, the paper should just hang there, but it did not. When he blew over top of the paper, the rest raised in his hands. I couldn't believe it. What a genius this Bernoulli guy was. I was hooked and wanted to know everything there was to know about aircraft. I was always impressed with flight operations, planes taking off and landing on this small airstrip manned by a bunch of eighteen-year-old kids running the flight deck. So at this point, I needed to know what made the whole thing work.

Every few weeks, we had a briefing by someone in our division, mostly junior intelligence specialists, about something having to do with naval operations, enemy capabilities or whatever was assigned. This was continuing education that would keep our study and briefing skills up to par if we were needed in some tasks down the road. I was given the Patriot missile system. We were patrolling the no-fly zone over Iraq since the active fighting stopped during Desert Storm. This was my opportunity to bring myself out of the quagmire my poor reputation put me in. Since Saddam Hussein had been firing Scud missiles at Israel a bit too much, the US had deployed the Patriot missile system to defend the only democracy in the region. I was excited to prove myself but had to start from scratch since I knew nothing about the protective missiles we had deployed to destroy Scud missiles.

I got to work each night after my twelve-hour shift was over. I gathered all the materials I could to learn about the missile system and put it into briefing form. Every briefing I had been witness to involved slides and someone either reading their notes or referring to their notes so much it was a distraction. I was determined to do the entire briefing from memory along with slides to support my message. After putting everything together, I wrote out the brief word for word and spent hours after my shift going over it again and again I briefed myself in a back room for hours, saying it repeatedly. The Scud missile system is a ballistic missile, which means it is not guided. They know how much fuel the system has and point it at an angle designed to strike whatever target based on how long the fuel will last. At that point, fuel runs out and gravity takes over to land the missile wherever that may be. The Patriot missile was designed to shoot down aircraft, so it was working beyond its design. The missile comes with a targeting partner that tracks unwanted airborne threats and assigns a target to each Patriot that is fired. It will guide the missile to where it is going, not to where it is at the moment. Anticipating where it would fall was the easy part; hitting such a small target was the challenge. There were also concerns that the Patriot would turn one target into many and fall to earth in pieces. Anyway, I briefed from memory; my junior enlisted in the back were falling asleep, but the brass was gleaming. I had finally improved their opinions of me; I had credibility. I was then assigned to Strike Plot, the most challenging office in the center, in my opinion. I was then named air order battle analyst, meaning it was my duty to track the goings-on of the Iraqi Air Force and pass that knowledge on to the admirals' intel officer called the N2.

I spent all my waking time learning everything I could get my hands on about the Iraqi Air Force: the type of planes they had, how many, and where they were based. I needed to know the capabilities of the aircraft as well as the training of the pilots. What were those planes armed with? What were the capabilities of those weapons and what were the limitations? All of it. I loved it. At some point, I got so good at briefing I didn't need a script. I memorized everything that had gone on the day before and passed on to CDR Tom Bortmes, the admirals' guy. I couldn't believe that a guy who couldn't remember anything in intel school was now memorizing everything he had to pass on in a matter of hours. I started a weekly air summary and got permission to pass on to the squadron-ready rooms on board. I was granted permission and began getting positive feedback from the pilots. Of course, they loved it; they wanted to know who they were going to blow away if attacked and where they would be coming from. I looked at these guys like they were professional athletes, and I was pleased that I could help them in their mission.

My job was incredibly satisfying, and I was also lucky to have Meat with me. Yes, Jim Baker who I knew in intel school was assigned to VF-213, an F-14 squadron. It was great having him with me, and he would tell me what to expect when I was new. Of course, he was assigned to a squadron, so he knew nothing about the ship. These guys were only there when the planes were. What a joke; while they were off on shore with sand between their toes, the ships' crew were cleaning, painting, or whatever else we were needed. It was great having him, but he couldn't help me with my sleeping problem.

Almost nightly, I would have dreams of being buried alive, being run down by a train or smashed up in the trunk of a car that was being demolished. The main problem was that I was acting out and actually sleepwalking. That is a no-no in the navy; they don't want some poor soul walking off the ship into the water, never to be heard from again. I can't put a number on how many nights I would scream, jump out of my rack, or dive under a table in my sleep. Since I had become a contributing member of the team, at first, these were overlooked. One night, however, Jim and I had gone out to the USO in the UAE (United Arab Emirates) and drank our faces off. I was drinking some foreign beer from Australia, I think. I didn't realize that the alcohol content on these things were double that of Coors Light or whatever I drank back home.

I knew I was banged up and decided to head back to the boat, a forty-five-minute trek with desert everywhere for the eye to see. Once back on board, I hit the rack. The next thing I knew, Fred Hyde was leaning out of his rack and yelling, "Hey, get Barratt!" I was peeing on a chair in birthing. Oh boy, now what? I was still intoxicated but coming out of it, but not by much when DP2 Kemp took me to medical. After swallowing anger and resentment at both my attacker and initial treatment on the boat, it all came rushing out. This took place while I was trying to establish myself, and I wasn't quite there, I think. I don't know, my time line memory is not all I would like it to be. Anyway, I began screaming at Kemp, taking all my balled-up anger out on him. To his credit, he took it with professionalism and knowledge that I was just drunk. This would lead to a psychological evaluation, however.

I don't remember the doctor's name or even if he was qualified in mental health, but I had some answering to do. He asked about my past drinking. At the time, I was just a casual drinker; yes, I had been a wild man in college, but even then was only two days a week or whatever. In intel school, Jim and I and another kid would grab a six-pack, and we found a spot where the Philadelphia Phillies broadcast could be listened to at night. I'd loved the Phillies since I was a kid and used to watch with my father. They won the World Series in 1980, lost in 1983, and then were killing it in 1993. They stunk for ten years, and now that I was in the navy, they decided to be great. Anyway, the review went well, and I was free to get back to work. At no point did I even consider sharing my wonderful experience in Alameda, no way. Case closed.

Near the end of our deployment in late September, we were on our way to port after being out to sea for three weeks or so when I noticed something weird on CNN International on our monitors in the office. Our guys were being dragged in the streets of Mogadishu, Somalia, with nothing more than their skivvies on. I was instantly in a controlled rage. We turned up the volume. They had explained that two of our helicopters were shot down, and the crew were captured and killed and now being humiliated on the world's stage. Even in war there should be decency, in my view. War is violent and ugly, and

I had only seen the aftermath, never the ugliness of it happening in real time. But even when you do take life in war, which is inevitable, decency should always be shown to the fallen enemy. What were these savages thinking? I remember one of my shipmates said, "I wonder how long it's going to be before we are headed down there." Sure enough, the ship started shaking; we had gone from ten knots to full power, which is somewhere in the area of thirty knots. The captain came over the 1MC, which is the ship's intercom. He informed us that we were headed to Somalia. We all wanted vengeance for our guys and were psyched to be headed down there. We had to get through the Strait of Hormuz, the only way to get in and out of the gulf.

The strait is only maybe a mile from the tip of the UAE and Oman to Iran on the other side. The *Abraham Lincoln* is 1,200 feet long as I've said, but also one hundred thousand tons. Going thirty-plus knots in a constricted waterway, we can't exactly hit the brakes at a moment's notice. I was ordered to get to the top of the island of the ship in case we hit someone. I would then take the specifics, write a report, and pass it up the chain of command. *That will never happen*, I thought. Oh, boy, there were two small fishing boats with motors on the back of the small craft trying to cross our path. These guys couldn't be this dumb, could they? Yes, they could. They kept their heading, and I was going to witness the death of four men, two per boat. The first boat made it safely, but I was sure we were going to destroy the dummy in the second boat. Well, off to Allah with you. The bridge lay on the horn five times, the international shipping code for "get out of the way, we are not stopping." I was sure this guy was done and went to the back of the island. He was alive, but he was a bit shook up; his boat was all out of whack, and he was desperately clinging to his boat to stay aboard. Just missed.

We got to Somalia two days later and were eager to make waste of the place. Nothing happened, however. We just took pictures and stopped dead a mile offshore to show the Somalis that they had woken a sleeping giant. It was disappointing. We wanted to do our duty to protect our guys and maybe give them a sting to never do this again. Apparently, President Clinton waved the white flag and shut down all operations. Interesting choice, which would later invite the biggest attack on our country on 9/11. My opinion, anyway.

I got back to Alameda and reunited with Marcy, who had to quit her job in New Jersey to move out to California. We kept busy renting an apartment and doing all the things it took to begin building a life. One other way I was naive was how often I would actually be out to sea. I thought we sail once every year or so for another six months. Not the case at all, actually. Should have not been so clueless, but being back from a cruise didn't mean the navy stopped. There were maintenance issues, refits of whatever needed to be replaced, and qualifying to get out to sea all over again. There was a set schedule to ensure there would be no problems once we head to sea again. We also had to qualify the air wing, which meant doing it at sea. Young pilots needed to be able to take off and land safely in order to get permission to join their squadron. Interesting process, actually. Watching the new guys try to land was a nerve-racking thing to witness. They were all over the place, trying to get to the deck. In our workspaces, we had TV monitors with an option to watch flight ops. It would be in black and white, with crosshairs on the monitor indicating where the planes needed to be positioned to land safely. Not easy I guess until they get the experience and confidence to do it on a regular basis. For our cruise coming up called WESTPAC (Western Pacific), we were qualifying the first women pilots assigned to our ship. They were very capable, as you can imagine, but were probably under more pressure than the men knowing they carried the hopes of other women behind them. The F-14 squadron had several women who happened to be very tall, all of them. One of them was Kara Hultgreen, a very positive and kind officer who was full of confidence and excitement as far as I could tell. I didn't know her well, only enough to say "good morning, ma'am" on the occasion she was in CVIC.

We were off the coast of San Diego in late 1994, I think. We were qualifying all the squadrons. I was in the head (bathroom) shaving to get up to work when I heard the call over the 1MC, "Plane in the water, plane in the water." Uh-oh. I rushed up to the intel center, and they were already watching the replay in our Mission Planning space. They rewound the tape and played it time and again.

She approached the fan tail (back of the ship) when her F-14 veered left and entered the water. You could see a flash of the eject packs that had sent both the pilot and radar intercept officer out of the plane. In the F-14, since there are two crew members, they have to eject away from one another to avoid an in-air collision. Unfortunately, at time of ejection, the aircraft was in an almost vertical position and Lt. Hultgreen was ejected directly into the water. They later found her body, still in her seat, at the bottom of the Pacific. Shame, she was a good one from what I could tell. The RIO got out safely without a scratch. Dangerous business these people are in.

My next cruise was fast approaching, and Marcy was not happy about it. Neither was I, but I figured we should get this over with. She had a job in Oakland at the federal courthouse and had settled in. Aside from the murders in broad daylight that she witnessed, everything was proceeding swimmingly. Oakland was lovely and right next door. I used to ride my bike to the base to avoid parking: gone. Hubcaps on our car (yes, we had hubcaps back then): gone. Oh well, let's move on.

It was around this point with the cruise imminent that I had the unique pleasure of meeting Ensign Perry Miller, a Naval Academy graduate and a complete bonehead. If I were tasked to build a more incompetent idiot and put an officer's uniform on him, I couldn't come close to this guy. I couldn't believe this guy was a ring wearer. How in the world did this guy not only get into Annapolis but also graduate? What did I care? I just needed to focus on my job. When time came to shove off, Marcy drove me to base in tears. I wasn't thrilled myself as I was leaving her home alone, no protection. By this time, we got a white German shepherd to scare off any potential troublemakers, so I relaxed a little. We left port, and off we went. Heading west, I focused on picking up where I left off in Strike Plot, getting everything in place to really make a difference this time. I had not a worry in the world as long as this Perry moron kept his distance.

About a week out, passing Hawaii, I heard the officers talking with Chief Hyde. They were going to… What were they saying? No, *no, no!* Yes, they assigned Ens. Moron to Strike Plot. Like Quint from

Jaws at the end trying to kick off the shark, there I was mentally fall-ing apart that this…man would be in my presence for six months. *Well,* I thought, *ensigns are harmless. They're even greener than I am, and they are usually very humble as they learn the goings-on around them.* I was a *big* third-class petty officer now, ha! I also had Lt. Dan Salyan, a Virginia Military Institute graduate and very capable offi-cer. My first run-in with him was not all that pleasant, but in time I came to appreciate his leadership and dedication.

On my first cruise, I got notice from a lawyer that I was being sued by a kid whose face I introduced my fist to at the local college bar two years earlier. The good news was that people couldn't sue service members while they were on active duty. The thought behind this was that the service member would not be around to defend them-selves; the suing party would have to wait until that man's service had ended. In my mind, I was in the clear; even if it was adjudicated, it would have to wait until I was home. Therefore, the navy didn't even have to know or deal with it. It didn't quite work out that way. I got the notice, told Randy Brown, asked him to keep it to himself, and he instantly took it into Cdr. Cobery's office and told everyone. What a guy, huh? Anyway, not only was I angry about Randy ratting me out before he could take his next breath; now a major meeting was about to take place. Like a congressional hearing televised live, I would be on the hot seat, and I couldn't plead the fifth. I kept tell-ing them that this matter was none of the navy's business; it didn't involve them! Not exactly a winning argument. Yeah, Lt. Salyan had seen and heard enough. Boy, was I stupid and cocky at the same time!

Back in a room able to fit about one man, four of us crammed in for what would come to be a relentless, viscous bashing of one RB. I really don't remember all that much. Lt. Salyan was one of those guys who either drank way too much coffee or had some nervous disorder that was never addressed. His legs bounced constantly, and he had permanent pit stains even right out of the shower. I thought he might have deodorant that was made of pure water. His voice was loud, but all I remember was, "I am so sick of hearing your name" and then an avalanche of insults with more four-letter words than I had ever been witness to. I took it well, I think. I realized how I came off, and it was beyond apologizing for. What I couldn't believe, though, was the carpet bombing of the f-word flung in my direction like arrows. I actually started to count, but it was worthless; they came too fast. After he stormed out of the room, I almost chuckled at how committed Lt. Salyan was at tearing me up. It was impressive, total talent. Chief Hyde stepped in like a true leader and gave me some compliments, maybe out of fear I would just jump into the ocean or something, and I appreciated it. I do remember him saying, "I don't want to paint too rosy of a picture here either." I thought, a second wave of F bombers were coming; more Ronnie bashing was clearly coming, but it didn't. I look back at this with fondness now, got to say, and I think it's hilarious. Anyway, I had the Miller challenge on my hands. What to do?

In case you are wondering, yes, I still had my sleeping issues and was still afraid to go to sleep. I just could not keep screaming and jumping out of my rack. This cruise, I had a secret weapon—alcohol. Alcohol was not allowed on board for obvious reasons. There were a billion moving parts on this behemoth of a ship, especially the flight deck. There was no room for anyone being impaired on the job. To me, however, I thought I had no choice. I needed to get through this cruise and see where the navy would take me. Convincing Marcy would have to be put on the bottom of the list right now. Back then, I was a beer drinker, and there certainly wasn't room for a small refrigerator and cases of beer. This wasn't college. Before we pushed off, I ran to the liquor store to find something white that would look like water. I got the biggest water bottle I could find for this dangerous idea. I'm sure you're assuming that I got vodka. Remember, we are talking about me here. You know, the same guy that missed his flight? Asked an obvious prostitute if she actually *was* a prostitute and couldn't color between the lines in intel school. No, I got sambuca. Yeah, sambuca. Just typing the word makes me have flashbacks at how awful this stuff was, especially over the course of three months, which is what it took me to finish it. It was tucked in my rack ready to help me get through each night.

*****

We stopped in Hong Kong and dropped anchor in the harbor. I couldn't believe how many small fishing boats there were around us, upward of one thousand if I had to guess. They had ferries running nonstop to take guys to and from the city. Now, others have said how incredible Hong Kong was. I thought it was a cesspool, pure and simple. It looked like what is Chicago or San Francisco now. People were openly relieving themselves in the streets and doing it like this was not only acceptable but encouraged. The smell was overwhelming. My heart goes out to San Diego and San Francisco folks who have to deal with this today. Navigating through the excrement minefield was interesting, I guess. Hey, join the navy and see the world! Let's go see hundreds of people pooing in the streets all at the same time! Delightful.

I'm not sure what other folks made, but my paychecks were in the area of $160 per week. We worked twelve hours on and twelve hours off seven days per week. If you do the math, I made $1.90 per hour. Not a complaint, just an observation. The point is that in Hong Kong, everything was off-the-rails expensive, so our choices in what to do were incredibly limited. I also struggled with the crowding in the streets. I didn't realize it until years later, but I always seemed distracted with finding the exits if I was in a restaurant, and I couldn't stand someone walking behind me. If I was in a restaurant, I needed my back to the way with at least two exits within quick reach. I also seemed to have a pressure in my chest, especially at night. I just wanted to get out of this place.

*****

Back to sea and on the way to Singapore and then the Indian Ocean on the way to the gulf, I began to really get into a rhythm. I worked nights, which I preferred because there were less people around. That left me in the office with three other guys and Ensign Miller, who was now LTJG (Lieutenant Junior Grade) Miller. Oh boy, that one pay grade pumped up his ego, and he was ready to become the tyrant he turned out to be. At the beginning of my twelve-hour shift, I would always go to the vending machines that the ship had.

There were about thirty machines with soda available for fifty cents apiece. I would grab two Mountain Dew, chug them, and head up to the office. I would then pour a large coffee in my mug that I brought along with me. Navy coffee is exactly what everyone has heard about; it's almost a solid, like a slow mud slide. And it is grade A jet fuel. I would pour half a cup and use water to fill the rest of my cup to avoid a heart attack that would come from the high concentration of caffeine. I would then get to Strike Plot and begin the day. I would go over each day's intelligence about the Iraqi Air Force, how many sorties, whether they were dogfighting or doing ground attack, and if they used live ordinance during training. There were other sources of intel throughout the night, and I had a great relationship with the air force in Riyadh, Saudi Arabia. At the time, the Internet was in its infancy stage, but we did have capability to "text" with the air force. There were two or three other sources of intel that would come in, just raw numbers. I didn't worry about Miller; he slept most of the night but would poke his head in from time to time.

Through the night, in preparation for presenting the day's activities to Commander Bortmes, I had to take all of this raw data and begin to put it together in a way that was conversational. I would get a chart of Iraq and plot the activity that went on: what kinds of planes, from where, and how many. I would also take the data and compare it to the year before to determine if the air activity was normal or indicative of something else. When Miller would poke his head in, he would disrupt the whole office, asking mundane questions and demanding answers to things that made zero sense. Where is so and so? What is he doing? Where are you going? How long are you going to be? During the night, my concentration was of a singular focus. I knew what I had to do and by when. By 3:00 a.m., I would need to be almost done with my written report and by 5:00 a.m., I would begin to wrap my head around what I needed to say. At 6:00 a.m., I would head back to the film imaging room and practice out loud, over and over and over again. By 7:00 a.m., I would be ready to give a detailed and professional briefing. Miller did everything he could to disrupt this entire process. Now, if he had something to add or something that needed my attention, of course, I would follow orders. But heading to the copier to make sure the senior officers all had a copy of what I was talking about and then him stopping me to ask how long it would take? My patience was running thin. "Where you going?" To the head, I would say. This idiot would then ask, "How long?" *What? Well, sir, at this juncture, I must report to you that this operation would consist of making potty, not a tinkle. Therefore, sir, I must admit that I cannot determine the duration of this operation, but I can assure you, sir, that I will exfiltrate the operation in a timely manner.* I couldn't believe this guy was an officer.

The only thing that would give me any mental relief was that he slept most of the night and give us all peace. He would also fall asleep during briefings every morning, and I mean *every morning.* I was so embarrassed for him sleeping in front of senior officers and other enlisted I would almost lose control. I wanted to cringe. I would use my pointer that I used during briefings and tap him under the table to wake him up. Future chief of naval operations sitting here. By then we also had women on board and our commander of the intelligence center was a distinguished woman by the name of Barbara Boyer. The lieutenant commander was a former enlisted man called John Sanford. On the first cruise in 1993, I remember a lot of guys were at each other's throats. Women came on board, and suddenly, the guys were on their best behavior. Classic. I didn't care; I enjoyed the calm that the women brought with them.

Now in the gulf, my job was more and more exciting and satisfying, and I couldn't put the stuff down. I made binders with information so that anyone cleared could get a picture of exactly what the Iraqi Air Force consisted of. Pictures, breakdowns of capabilities, and anything else I could think of. The only issue I really had was sleeping. By now, we shared a birthing compartment with two hundred other guys, and it was flat-out challenging. Since I worked nights and the other guys didn't care, the sound could be deafening at times. Doors slamming, guys just standing there having conversations, and turning the lights on from time to time made sleeping a monster effort. Since I had trouble sleeping from my uninvited staff sergeant in Alameda, I was lucky to have booze on board. I would go and get two diet Coke and pour half out and fill it up with my sambuca. I would then sip two drinks while writing letters or listening to music. I also was forced to have earplugs in and wrap my eyes up to block out the light. Nothing is easy in the navy, not even sleep. After two hours or so, my drinks would be gone, and I could feel the tension leave me. Off to sleep I went. I didn't need an alarm clock at this point; my body just seemed to know when to get up. I would shower, shave, dress, and off to my Mountain Dew waiting for me. Twelve-hour shift, rinse, and repeat.

By now, my friend Ray Kemp was gone, and with it our deep conversations about the state of current affairs. He was a gift to me, and I missed our conversations and the connection we shared. Randy proved to be a friend in Kemp's place. He knew so much about the navy he was a source of information for my never-ending curiosity. Randy also had his enlisted wings, which I wanted. Enlisted wings mean that the sailor wearing them are air warfare qualified. The program consists of constant reading and getting hundreds of signatures from other sailors who already had their wings. In order to qualify, I needed to know everything about naval aviation—how a plane flies, how a helicopter flies, what the control surfaces that control the aircraft are, what maintenance is like, where the safety crews on areas of the ship are. Anything you can think of about flight operations, I needed to have committed to memory. I submitted a written request to begin the program. I was told many times that no E-4 had their wings on the ship and most guys who started never finished *Well, thanks for that. Now I know I'll finish.* It would normally take six months from what I was told. I had no interest in taking six months. I spent hours studying, getting signatures, and setting appointments with other qualified sailors. Well, in keeping with Ron Barratt tradition, I fouled it up. At the end of the program, an oral board was the last step. I remember a chief asking where the fire stations were on the ship. I completely overthought the whole thing. I didn't know the space numbers, which, of course, was not what he was asking. He was asking me in general. There were fire stations on a carrier on the flight deck, the hangar bay, the island, the bow, and fan tail. What a twit I was. I rescheduled and passed the second time and was now air warfare qualified.

The reason this was so important to me was, first, I loved and still love aviation, but second, it meant instant credibility to anyone who saw them. In the military, everyone you meet for the first time will look at your shoulder and your chest to determine what kind of person you are, what rank, and how many medals. I wasn't crazy about that, but it was the norm at the time. If someone met me for the first time, they would see my wings and think that maybe I was a squared away sailor.

I still had Miller to deal with, and he consistently ramped up his ridiculous behavior. He had no idea how to lead or how the office worked since he slept through most of it. He may also have been offended by my growing confidence. I was probably cocky or arrogant to a degree. I don't know. He began to ride me in a way that I truly resented. If I walked on one side of the office to the other, he wanted to know why. If I ran to the copier or anywhere else, he was there to needle me. My patience was running thin because I could detect a certain level of joy he got at angering me. He became an incompetent bully. One night, as I was in total focus about my job and oblivious to my surroundings, once again I heard him babbling about something. I realized it was directed toward me. Before I could think, I blurted out, "Sir, if you want to know what is going on in this office, maybe you should spend a bit more time here." Not a good idea. I challenged the authority of an officer. As I tried to remove myself from a heated situation in an effort to keep it from escalating, he ordered me to stop. I did. He came out to the passageway and cut off my escape and said in a very aggressive way, "I'm not done with you." I was now in a rage, and I visualized blasting this guy in his face and beating him. I certainly couldn't' do that. I needed to escape a dangerous situation and go blow off steam. The chart room.

The intel center had a chart room the size of a garage about fifty feet away, and that's where I headed. No one should be there, and I could freely yell and scream and get this out of my system while at the same time avoiding getting into any type of trouble. The chart room had thousands of classified charts of the entire world and had a cypher lock to limit entry. I hit the buttons necessary and expected relief. That expectation was crushed when I looked down and one of my shipmates was in there organizing the room. In complete frustration and anger, I started crying and went to the back of the room. I was trapped with nothing to help me get this frustration out. I punched the safe in front of me. *Great, my hand is broken. Way to go, Barratt.*

I looked at my hand and knew it was broken. I had to face the fire. I gathered myself up, made sure my uniform was squared away, and headed to see Chief Hyde. Chief Hyde is a unique man. I never in my life saw a man in the zone more than him. He was all business and without emotion. Not much impressed him, and yet no crisis was a crisis to him, just an issue to be dealt with. I poked fun at him from time to time, and at the desk watch, I drew a picture of him standing there with the stoic look on his face that he always seemed to have. In a way to shed light on his ability to never be impressed, the caption said, "Chief, you just won a million dollars." "Keep it, I have work to do." Another caption I put in there was "Chief, Cindy Crawford is at the front desk and says she wants to meet you!" "Is she cleared?" It's still funny to me now; it just illustrates his overall demeanor at all times at work. Anyway, I was confident that, one, I had to cop to this idiotic mistake I made. And two, I was sure he would just tell me to keep calm and should get this behind us. That's exactly what happened. I gave him a brief outline of the situation and how I handled it poorly. He told me to get to medical, get it fixed, and then head back up. I did.

When I came back up to CVIC, I was invited to speak to Cdr. Sanford in his office. John Sanford, as I stated earlier, was a former enlisted guy who had made a successful career in the navy and now was an O-4. He was also bipolar as far as I could tell. I never saw a guy go from being incredibly positive to a downright meltdown in the course of seconds. I was nervous. He was professional and asked me about the situation in Strike Plot. I guess since I had gained some kind of credibility in the eyes of the brass, my opinion mattered. I was honest but also completely humble and willing to take whatever responsibility for my actions that were required. This was my fault. He said, "We are not going to send you to Captain's Mast."

Captain's Mast is like a municipal court dealing with small crimes that amount to misdemeanors. Some form of punishment would be handed down to those who find themselves in front of the captain, who was Robert Willard at the time. He was a former F-14 pilot and now ran the ship, an incredibly impressive man I had the pleasure of meeting in my office when he was transitioning to take command. He had asked me direct questions about the Iraqi Air Force, and I answered directly. He was going to be a great commander of the ship. I would rather not meet him in this instance, and John Sanford had told me that was not going to happen. I was confused, however, why I would have to go to mast. I damaged government property, I was told.

"The safe is fine," I responded.

"No, Petty Officer Barratt, *you are damaged government property*." That was an eye-opener to me. I never considered myself property, interesting. That was the moment I began questioning if I had a future in this navy. I had decided against BUD/S. I knew I couldn't stand the cold water for more than eight seconds, and I wasn't crazy about jumping out of airplanes. I had done it once, and it was not pleasant. Those guys are special, and they know it. They are the ones who go through hell, intentionally and deliberately. They deserve whatever attitude they choose to have. I really wanted to be a part of something so special. I had the will, running, and physical ability. Not enough, though. While we sleep comfortably at night, SEALs are leaving their families at a moment's notice, off to some disgusting part of the world with an expectation that they won't come back. They agree that they are expendable assets. Crazy impressive men. I just didn't have what it took to join them. Anyway, I digress. At this point, I also had to take into consideration that this would be on my record forever, maybe. I had no idea what would be recorded or not.

I later found out that the brass, the serious brass, began asking questions about the cause of my loss of control. They had to know that Miller was a strange guy. He fell asleep right in front of all of them at every briefing. What they didn't know, however, was that he was driving the entire office crazy with me leading the pack. Now

I had to deal with the dishonor of having a cast on my arm for six weeks.

At the back end of our time in the gulf, I was told that I was heading to Qatar, the island nation in the gulf very close to the coast of Saudi Arabia. Qatar had relaxed ways of doing things, unlike Saudi Arabia. Alcohol was available, and they had an open-arms approach to the United States. I was being sent there to liaison with the air force that was based there. I had a job to do, or so I thought. I flew off the ship on a CH-53, which is enormous and can hold fifty sailors, if I had to guess. When I landed, I was taken to a hotel with armed guards surrounding the building. I was shown to my "room." This place was gigantic and was big enough to fit a family of five. I was a bit confused but prepared to report to the air force in the morning. When I got there the next day, it was nothing more than a trailer. Two airmen were in there and took about ten minutes to show me the operation.

"What do you need me to do?" I asked.

I was told to go sit by the pool and have a beer. I was confused and uncomfortable like I was doing something wrong. It dawned on me that my command sent me there for some time to myself. I was grateful and shocked but still appreciative. Sit by the pool, huh? It was 115 degrees out, and the water was over 100. *I don't think so.* I grabbed a few movies, yes, VHS and headed to my room.

That night I decided to head out to a bar and have a few beers. I jumped in a cab, and he dropped me off. Not too friendly, I thought of the cab driver, but who cared? I was half done with my first beer when something occurred to me. *What am I doing?* I was in a foreign country, alone, and had no idea where I was. We didn't have cell phones back then; I could flat-out disappear at a moment's notice. Once again, Barratt was a twit. The same cab driver was out there, and I asked if he would take me back to the hotel. I was in a mentally defensive posture. How many times had we been told never to go anywhere alone? This wasn't some cushy small town in Indiana or anything. All workers like cab drivers or waiters were from unfriendly countries like Pakistan or Afghanistan. The cab driver kept looking at me in the rearview mirror. My heart was racing. *Is this guy going to pull down some alley and have five guys waiting for me?* The only thing I could think at this point was how committed this guy was. *Dude, are you really committed? I'm all in, so you'd better believe in your mission with everything you got if you mean me harm.* I began visualizing different scenarios and me beating this guy to a pulp. I also could be completely mistaken, but then, why did he keep looking at me? Probably not a great idea, but I blurted out, "If you're thinking about taking me somewhere to meet your buddies, just remember, I'm killing you first." Paranoid, I think. He spoke broken English, and I was not sure he got the translation, but he did see my body language. I got back safe. Disaster averted, or the beginning of mental illness. *Err on the side of safety*, I thought.

Back on the ship, every night, I prayed for my parents. *Please, Lord, protect my parents while I'm out to sea.* The military is not all that lovey-dovey when it comes to service members losing loved ones. Fly back home, go to the funeral, fly back, and get to work. That was what I was told anyway. Every night, same prayer. We were headed back, and I looked forward to really having a life with my wife. During my second tour, I had my paychecks directly deposited to her so she could pay the bills. It was a normal and obvious thing to do. I think it caused problems later on, but at the time, it was necessary. The ship was headed to the yards in Bremerton, Washington, upon our return, and while on the way, I started thinking about my future. I was coming up to the end of my enlistment, and I needed to make a decision. The chain of command had been asking, and rightfully so, about my intentions to reenlist or not. I pushed them off, telling them I was considering it. I knew I had a challenge convincing Marcy that I could make an impact on any command that I was assigned to, and I really wondered what limits, if any, I had. I also wanted to know my options. I had a college degree; therefore, I was qualified to at least try for a commission. I also had the option of staying in the enlisted ranks and pursuing khakis.

I went to my LPO, Randy, and asked his opinion. He told me I would never make chief because I had broken my hand and that, that incident would follow me around like a dark shadow the rest of my time in the navy. I went to Cdr. Sanford and asked about becoming an officer. I was coming up to a promotion that I was confident I would get, and that was second class petty officer or the equivalent of a sergeant in the army. If I got that promotion, I was confident that I could convince Marcy we had a future and that the navy would be signaling to me that they had plans for me. Commander Sanford told me without any hesitation that I would not become an officer, not now, at least. He told me that the navy stopped that sort of program and that I would be better off getting out and applying for the FBI. I had hit a wall. I was told I had a mediocre future ahead of me, at best, by both Randy and Sanford. I decided to get out.

By the time we headed to Bremerton, Randy had left for his next adventure, as well as Fred Hyde. Dan Salyan was rotating off the ship as well and had a dilemma before he left. He was assigned to the mine warfare planning program. The mine warfare program was a daunting task that he would rather not do because transitioning off the ship would take up most of his time. He had to check out of almost every department on the ship: medical, personnel, and so forth. He openly questioned how he could do both. I told him I would do it, with his permission. I figured it would get me out of chipping and tiling, and I could sit in a quiet room and blast this out. I had no idea what I got myself into.

The mine warfare program was comprised of about fifty target folders that outline how to lay minefields anywhere in the world. We had helicopters that could do it, as well as the S-3 Viking fixed-wing aircraft. Within these fifty folders, there were about one hundred classified charts of the topography of any given area in the world. I had to take inventory, identify what was missing, and get the required charts that needed to be in the package. In the navy, certain tasks are assigned to specific ranks, depending on the complexity of the situation. This job required an O-3 at a minimum or a lieutenant. I was an E-4, the equivalent of a corporal in the army. This was way above my pay grade. Lt. Salyan let me take the reins anyway.

I went to a back room and began taking apart each folder. I had a list on me of required materials, and I would check off each one that was there in an effort to find the missing items. This was going to take a month and a half, I thought. I had two weeks, if I recall correctly. Lt. Salyan would poke his head in periodically and ask how I was doing. I jokingly told him I wanted the Medal of Honor for this one. After I finally identified what was needed to complete the required inventory, I realized I had a problem. These charts are all classified, and I needed to contact the Defense Intelligence Agency to get them filled. The problem was, I was a junior enlisted intelligence analyst. Why would they respond to me? Answer? They wouldn't. I got major pushback in the beginning.

They asked, "Who are you and why are you in charge of this program at your rank?"

How could I answer? I peppered the DIA with phone calls in the hopes of getting someone else to answer. I got lucky a few times and had charts mailed by classified courier. I was about 30 percent done. I had Lt. Salyan call on my behalf. That proved fruitful, another 30 percent down. I had to call other agencies as well, and each time a delivery was made, I had to track down the chart number and find out where it belonged. Toward the end, with time running out and Salyan almost out of here, I asked if our sister ship, the USS *Carl Vinson* might have the charts we were missing. The *Vinson* was moored directly across from us. We "borrowed" the charts we needed and completed the inventory. The last thing I did was put in a directory on the inside of the introductory folder. It told anyone who needed a specific chart where to find it and included a checkout sheet for chain of custody purposes. Exhausted, I dove in my rack. I had no idea that a full commander would be there hours later to inspect our work. He wrote that it was the finest organized and complete mine warfare program he had seen to date. I was awarded the Navy Achievement Medal, something I am still very proud of.

*****

Now that I was home with Marcy, I had a challenge in front of me—how to convince her I was considering the next step in the navy, and I needed her approval. Didn't go well. She wanted not a second more of this life. We drove to Washington State with our dog and a packed car. We settled in an apartment in Port Orchard, Washington, and tried to adjust to the change. As I went about becoming a professional tiler and painter, Marcy began to slip into depression. She was up all night, slept during the day, and had nothing more to do than to go for a run on occasion. She was always an avid runner, and we had a treadmill wherever we went. This didn't help her mental condition, however. She began to gain weight and sleep all day. One day with about eleven months left in my enlistment, she announced she was leaving and heading home. The federal courthouse in Trenton, New Jersey had offered her the old job she had before she left, and she wanted to take it. I was shaken a bit since I thought we were in this together. I was wrong and forced to face the final year alone.

This presented problems because of my fear of sleeping at night. I also wasn't sure what this meant for my marriage. I thought it was strange she wanted to leave so bad, but at the same time, she didn't want to tell the courthouse to wait a year either. Now I was alone. Nights were troubling, and I needed five beers to even relax a little and allow myself to sleep. After about five months, I was bumped to second class and had my second stripe. Now I was in charge of a crew of eight guys ordered to refit birthing areas. There were two layers of tile on the decks at this point, and the ship required we remove them both instead of adding another. The weight would cause problems. Each morning, we assembled in the CVIC for our daily bashing by Sanford. I've never seen a more negative and miserable person before or since. Each morning, we were told we were the worst division he had ever seen and that we would clearly fail at getting each job done. Another division would have to bail us out. Weeks went by with this lovely message. By the time we got to our workspace, my guys were always angry, and a complaint fest would ensue. "Who does Sanford think he is?" "Has he ever chipped this much tile and hauled it off a ship?" The complaining began to wear me down. It was the first time I had been in a leadership position in the navy and wasn't all that sure how to handle it. I still had a major problem with abuse of authority. In this instance, Sanford could say whatever he wanted. I didn't agree with the "you stink, prove me wrong" type of leadership, but I had a plan.

The next morning, I asked Sanford if we could have a blood-drive type chart so we could see and judge our progress. We had roughly 350 jobs to do, and based on the number completed, that would be illustrated on the chart. If we kept our schedule, he could not claim we were awful. Once my team and I got to our workspace, we had to remove all tile, replace it, and then paint the entire space. We had two weeks. Sanford was still going on and on how terrible we were, and my guys were at their wits' end. I gathered them together, told them that we all signed up for intel, but we were sailors first; this was only part of the job. If the navy wasn't for them, I said, there was nothing that anyone could do to stop time, and their time to leave would come. In the meantime, I gave each of them two minutes to complain. When they were done, I said we should get the job done in one week, not two. It happened, and the rest of the time, we all did our jobs professionally and quickly. We finished two months ahead of schedule.

When we were done with the jobs given to our division, of course, my guys thought we would kick our feet up and sit around for two months. At this time, I was told that I was going to have to report to the USS *California*, a cruiser, for a three-week deployment. What? I was told that the first class had chronic seasickness and was being transitioned out of the navy. I couldn't believe that a guy in the navy for that period of time was seasick. How had he managed before? Or had he never been to sea? Either way, three weeks went by, and I was finished with an interesting time on a smaller ship. It was time to let my chain of command know that I would be leaving the navy.

I let everyone know that I had chosen to move on to a different path. Sanford cornered me. It was very unusual for such a high-ranking officer to debrief an enlisted person of my rank. I sat down, very nervous about what was going to be said. For fifteen minutes, he crushed me. I was disloyal and an embarrassment. How could I leave after he *gave me my Navy Achievement Medal?* Wow, what a crazy insult. When I was in charge of the mine warfare program, I never saw this guy. Now he was claiming he convinced his superiors to just give it to me. I couldn't wait to leave. The day I checked out, I ripped my uniform off and drove home in my skivvies. I was free to go. I drove home from Washington State to New Jersey. Next chapter, but what now? After the visit from my marine friend in the middle of the night, I had been so busy I never gave it a moment of thought even though I had trouble with sleeping, mild paranoia, and a problem with abusive authority. I had dealt with the situation with alcohol. That would only get worse, much worse.

BACK HOME

When it was time to leave Bremerton, Chris Bottcher and I loaded up my Nissan Pathfinder, and we began to head east. We really had no idea how long it would take. I was discharged, but Chris was on leave, or vacation, so he didn't want to waste too much time. The first incredible memory was driving east on Route 90. It was night, and beyond my headlights, I couldn't see a thing. We had been driving off and on for what seemed like a lifetime. I had no idea where we were. The sun started to come up, and an outline to my left began to show a shape. I looked to my right and saw a sign ahead that said, "Welcome to Wyoming." I slammed the brakes and stopped directly at the sign. The sun was on its way up to the sky now. I got out of the car and looked; it was a huge mountain range beginning to show itself. I stood there for a second. I could have been the only person on earth right now. I couldn't believe how quiet it was, and beautiful. As I stood there, my only thought was, *There must be a God. This doesn't happen by accident.* I took a picture. Awe-inspiring view. This was 1996, so there were no cell phones at the time, and of course, I lost the picture, but I will forever remember that moment.

After we got back and said our goodbyes, Marcy and I found a house that we could rent on the property of our landlords. The house was wonderful, and we were excited. She was working at the Trenton Federal Court, and I began looking for a job. The state police were still in a hiring freeze, and I had to find out how best to earn a living. I had no ideas. The other issue was that the tightening of my chest was back, especially when the sun went down. Add to that elevated heart rate and a sense of being trapped. I had no idea what would cause such a thing, but it was nothing that a six-pack of beer wouldn't fix. I started looking in the classifieds for a job. Yes, classifieds; hard to believe, I know. I noticed that some armored car service was hiring and went in for an "interview." I filled out the forms, passed the background check, and was hired in the course of a week. At the same time, I got a job pumping gas not far from the house. In New Jersey, your gas is pumped for you. I also got my coaching position back at Princeton High School that I had to say goodbye to when I left for the navy. I was busy.

I began to notice that the anger I carried with me on the ship didn't go away. I was aware of it without realizing its cause, and I decided to ignore it. Things would improve when I got a decent, full-time job. The armored car job was without any problems in the beginning. We would load up the cash needed for the banks and departments stores and head east on Route 195 toward the shore. We had scheduled stops, and as a driver, I had to stay with the vehicle at all times. It was a bit monotonous, but I dealt with it by reading. In the navy, I had developed a taste for reading since there wasn't much else to do and had begun a lifelong interest in American history books. We would get back to the yard at around 2:00 p.m. each day, and I would head home. I would head to football practice and pump gas around 6:00 p.m. to whatever time I was done. Things were going okay, and I settled into my routine. Not exactly what Marcy had in mind for a husband, I suspect. She wanted someone with a $500,000-per-year job that could take away her chronic anxiety. She never verbalized it, but money would become a monster focus of hers, and I suspect it still is. Why she married me, I couldn't tell you. If money was that important, then I wasn't the guy. I always wondered why she was so excited we were getting married. She knew exactly who I was, what I was doing, and that I would be serving on a ship somewhere. Without the help of some rich friend or something, what you see is what you get. I couldn't understand the unspoken disappointment. Did she think I was going to snap my fingers and become a neurosurgeon overnight or something?

The armored car company began to become a problem. This was a low-paying job ($8.50 at the time, I think) with nothing but men around each other at all times until the trucks were loaded, and off for the day they went. There were some issues that would pop up here and there almost daily. Guys would stick their chests out, and they would get into a testosterone contest. The constant bickering was wearing me down. That was when I was introduced to a slovenly, sloppy guy who thought he was Dirty Harry or some hero police officer. You know you're just a fat slob with a pistol on your waist, right? Always wanted to say that but never did. This guy was very impressed with himself, and he liked to let me know he was in charge. This wasn't going to end well. When we would break for lunch, I had some lame sandwich I slapped together last minute and a can of soda. This guy insisted on eating at Wendy's every day, and I mean *every day*. He told me he had stock in Wendy's, and he was trying to keep the business going toward a company he owned shares in. *Uh-huh, or maybe it's just that you're a gigantic slob who has an intimate relationship with a double cheeseburger.* I'd never seen a guy who have what looked like an intimate experience with food before. Absolute joy and pleasure with each bite of that giant, disgusting burger he shoved in his gullet. I would almost vomit every time we stopped and started to get out of the truck so I could stop fantasizing about bashing this guy in the face. Oh, and he chewed with his mouth open. Made me furious. I had a problem brewing with this anger I was carrying.

One day, I drove with two guards—the squared away guy I normally drove with and the Wendy's lover. Early on in the day, big boy seemed to want to impress the guy I usually drove with and had a decent working relationship. He did this by throwing verbal daggers in my direction.

"Hey, little guy, stay in the truck and don't j——k off. Didn't I tell you to organize the bags toward the back of the truck?"

After a few hours with him and his degrading comments, I started to fire back. "When is your next marathon? Didn't I see you on a fitness video? How long have you been bodybuilding? Instead of investing in Wendy's, you'd be better off investing in Scott toilet paper."

With each jab I threw his way, the more he wanted to put me in my place. He was in the jump seat in the back and didn't have his seat belt on. Before he could get his next insult out, I slammed on the brakes, sending him flying. At this point, I was ready for battle; I truly wanted to hurt him. We got back to the shop, and I quit on the spot. I didn't want to get into trouble and simply removed myself from the situation.

Nights were starting to really bother me at this point. I would drink the normal six-pack to get rid of the pressure in my chest, but I started attacking things in my sleep. One night, I guess I was half-asleep and saw a man in our bedroom with a rifle in his hand. I got up and tackled the intruder. Marcy put on the lights, and I had tackled the lamp in our room. We just tossed it up to a nightmare or something and ignored it. This was the second time this happened, as it began in Alameda when we were getting ready to move to Washington. I couldn't tell you what caused it. I never gave the marine a second thought, and I believed I was over that incident.

Since Marcy's brothers were so wonderful and successful at working in the stock market, I decided to impress her and do it myself. This meant I had to be a licensed broker and pass the Series 7. This was the financial sector's bar exam of sorts. I started at Paine Webber in Princeton. They paid a much better training salary than driving an armored car, that's for sure.

I began studying for the Series 7, and I have to say I wasn't picking it all up as fast as I would have liked. Options were the main culprit at this point. I kept getting the strike prices backward. I kept studying. At the time, I was hired with an attorney who had passed the bar but decided to attack Wall Street. We got along very well, but he wasn't taking the Series 7 seriously. He had passed the bar; the Series 7 was child's play. At the same time, we had to travel to Manhattan for formal training. We took the train every day and would end each trip at the World Trade Center. After about a month, we were scheduled for the exam. I thought, for me, it would be close. Looking at my buddy, though, his face was beet red; he knew he should have studied. We both failed. I missed by three points. It didn't matter; we were both let go. Time to regroup.

I have no idea how I got introduced to my next job interview, but a couple of weeks later, I was in Marlton, New Jersey, at Olde

Discount Stockbrokers. I really didn't think I had a chance since I failed the entrance exam. I simply explained that I was bothered by failure and wanted another shot. After becoming very good at briefing in the navy, I thought I would do well in presentations. The product didn't matter. I just needed to learn what I was selling, and off I would go. I also remembered that I had a hard time learning from just reading, so this time, I would go into an empty room and brief myself every day. I passed the test easily.

I can't tell you how much fun it was working at Olde. The technology market was starting to roar because of to the Internet stocks. All a company had to do to make money in an Initial Public Offering was have .com after their name. At twenty-eight years old, I was a bit older than most of the guys, and it was a blast. I had proven myself to the whole room that I had a knack for talking to people, and the branch manager took me as his assistant. He had given me a list of customers who hadn't bought a thing in over a year and gave me a mutual fund to learn. After about an hour going over the mutual fund, I came out and went down the list, calling every customer with a script in my head that was ready to be unleashed. After about my twentieth call, I got a customer on the line who hadn't bought anything for years. He had thousands of dollars sitting in the money market making 1 percent or whatever it was on his money. After my phone call, he put $50,000 in the mutual fund. Great sale. I would never talk to him again since my manager, Mike, now had an active customer.

The guys I worked with were very talented, and I would borrow sales tactics off anyone who said anything that I thought would be helpful to me. All young guys, all in white dress shirts, all positive and hungry guys. It was fantastic. After each day, I would be charged up and across the street we would go to the local pub. By then, the beer I was drinking every night had crept up in volume; I was up to maybe eight beers at night. I would catch a buzz and back to work; cold-calling I would go. It was successful, but at this point, I am willing to bet every broker in the country was successful. People would call during the day and ask for a random broker. I picked up the phone more than once to hear a guy ask me to buy $25,000 worth of some stock I never heard of before. Money was good, which meant things at home were good. I was content. Two storms were coming, and I got blindsided by both of them.

On March 10, 2000, the tech bubble burst, and we started hemorrhaging client assets. The word at the time was to hold and not give in to market pressures. After all, there had never been a crash that the market hadn't corrected and come back, ever. That wasn't good enough for our clients, though, and we started selling off like everyone else. People were furious that we didn't see this coming. My crystal ball was jammed, I told people. I used to get yelled at by people if a stock *only* went up three points in a day. I used to get phone calls saying, "XYZ was up 50 percent today. How come we didn't buy that?" Really? Hey, Bill, what's going to go up 50 percent tomorrow? I don't know. What makes you think *I do*? I really had a great time and learned a ton from the experience and the guys I worked with. But I got a phone call from my dad one night and was flattened at what he told me.

"Ronnie, I just want to tell you some news, and it's not all bad, so I don't want you to get upset. I have cancer." The blood came out of my face, and I couldn't breathe.

"What kind of cancer?" I asked.

"Non-Hodgkin's lymphoma, but it doesn't matter," he said. "It's the slowest growing cancer there is, and that will give us time to get rid of it." God love this man; I never heard a negative word come out of his mouth. He never cursed, never drank, and was always incredibly positive. "Things work themselves out, Ron. They always do." I heard this over a thousand times in my day, and I wish I could hear them a thousand more. My father was the most positive person I ever met. He was a gifted athlete who never boasted—two tryouts with the Phillies, began playing tennis for the first time in his thirties and got good quick. He was a Glassboro High School Athletic Hall of Fame inductee years before. He was a gentle father who would correct me with a look only. The message was always clear. When my mother and I would butt heads, he would sit on my bed and say nothing. I always knew never to be disrespectful in his presence to anyone. Nothing ever bothered him, to my knowledge, so if things bothered me, I kept quiet. Dad never had any interest in local politics and never formed any kind of coalition for him to benefit. He was kind to everyone always. He had an infectious sense of humor that drew people to him. My father was incredible, and now he was in trouble.

When Marcy got word of this, we wanted to have a son or daughter who would meet my dad. We started trying for a family. That would prove to be difficult. It was not happening. I prayed to our heavenly Father to bless us with a child. I went to a urologist for answers. Of course, that meant giving a donation, which was incredibly awkward. Once analyzed, I was told I was barely capable. I guess the powerful antibiotics that I had been given when I was sick at eight years old caused this. Who knows? Now what? Marcy started medication to make things easier, and lo and behold, she was pregnant. No coincidences. I was doing the math in my head. If the baby came, he or she would be about two years old at the four-year mark, the timeline the doctors had given Dad for his cancer. When we found out it would be a boy, we were ecstatic. At the time, my brother's son, Bobby, had been diagnosed with glioblastoma, a terminal brain cancer that cannot be destroyed. My brother's son was nine. At the time, I prayed often. Isn't that what most Christians do? We go about our lives ignoring the Lord, but in times of need, there we are knocking at His door. I prayed many times a day for the Lord to save my godson and my father; please, Lord!

In April of 1999, my son was ready to join us. We went to a hospital in Trenton for Marcy to bring my son into the world. I was so excited and incredibly scared at the same time. Keep in mind that I was naive and stupid. I had no idea it would take as long as it did. During the waiting periods, Marcy was in discomfort, and I felt like I had done something wrong. I felt guilty for causing my wife pain and suffering; it was almost unbearable. We started talking about names. We had come down to three names: Justin, Jason, or Brendan. That could wait. Marcy developed preeclampsia, a dangerous high blood pressure situation. I think I had my first cell phone by then and told my in-laws. They were on the way. After eighteen hours, Brendan joined us. I still felt awful for Marcy, but hey, look at my boy! They threw him on a hot plate and were manhandling him. I was a bit freaked out, but they wanted to get him crying so he would breathe on his own. Is it possible I got to this point in my life this ignorant? I instantly loved this little guy. *Wow!* I'm a dad! Brendan Michael Barratt joined us on April 13, 1999.

As a Christian, I speak to many people about a relationship with the Lord. You can't just join a gym and expect muscles without actually working out. Before there was a drop in the ocean or a star in the sky, Jesus loved you. All you have to do is love Him back. It is a mutual relationship to love the Lord and let Him lead you down the right path.

"How do you know you love Him?" they ask.

I ask them, "When your first child was born, how long did it take you to love him?" Instantly, I'm told. Okay, why? You didn't know him yet. He hadn't made you laugh or proud. The only thing he could do at the moment was breathe and cry, yet you loved him right away. With love, you just know and don't care about the reason. You don't have to explain it to anyone or talk about it. All you know is you love him, and that will direct your actions instinctively to do the right thing for your kids. The same goes for Jesus Christ. Give yourself to Him and you will experience a love you have never felt before. Amen?

At this point, we owned our first home, and I had made a change to a more well-known firm with more resources. I started at Janney Montgomery Scott on Market Street in Philadelphia. The stock market had slowed considerably, and it was not all that easy to convince clients at a discount firm to join me at a full-service firm. That meant full-service commissions. E-Trade and others were in their infancy, but the Internet was going pretty strong at the time. That meant potential clients who thought they knew more than they did, although they did know their stuff pretty well. Things were going well but slow, and I was working my tail off to make a living that would please my wife. My day consisted of taking the train across the bridge and walking six blocks to the office, checking headlines of the *Wall Street Journal* (there was never time to actually read it unless a headline jumped off the page), checking my positions and the news on each company that I recommended. At 9:00 a.m., I would hit the phones and begin cold-calling. I had written my own script and had perfected it. I ranked leads from A to D. An A lead meant they were ready to move then, and D leads were junk leads or someone to drip on with mailers.

I kept a log of the number of dials, contacts, and leads every day. I made sure to dial at least 150 times per day, and I would average five quality leads out of that. Not much on a percentage basis, but consistent. I was enjoying myself; it was the first time that I was my own boss. I never had anyone breathing down my neck as was the case at Olde. Looking back, I couldn't handle sales managers. They weren't putting in the work as I was. All they did was say, "We need more commissions, more sales." Really, I never thought of that genius. Any other gems of wisdom you would like to let me know about? Listen, a goal without a plan is a wish. Telling me where you want me to be and not offering *how* to get there isn't leadership; it's whining. So go back to your office and wait for your next bonus. Jeez, idiot managers were everywhere I went. I spent twelve hours a day cold-calling, and after 9:00 p.m., sometimes I would dial California or a different time zone. By this time, I was getting more and more worn out with making so little. I worried every day about how I was going to pay the mortgage every month. I started drinking vodka, and by now I had a bottle in my desk. Since I was always the last person in the office, I was free to do as I pleased. One challenge that nagged at me was Marcy. She would call me at my desk almost nightly and tell me how terrible things were and that she needed help.

"Help do what?" I asked.

"The dishes are piling up, and I'm trying to take care of Brendan," she said. Really? Do you want me to pay the mortgage or do the dishes?

After leaving at 9:30 p.m. or so, I would head to the train to get home. Each night there were folks who needed a helping hand. Since most of the time all I had was $5, I would give it to them. I would leave the next night; same guy waiting with the same story. *Sorry, bud, you got me last night.* There was an interesting guy whom I would meet on the street almost nightly. It was cold at the time, and this guy had found one grate in the city that blew dry heat, not steam. I would sit with him for thirty minutes or so and learn his story. He told me he had kidney problems, lost his family, and would hustle on the streets for enough money to get a motel room so he could shower. He didn't have a sales pitch, just down on his luck a bit. I helped him out as much as I could, and I began to like this guy. I asked him what he needed, and he told me "underwear and socks, sneakers if you have a used pair you're not using." No problem. I gave him what I could and gave him money when I had it. One night, I mentioned that I knew a guy who ran a car wash, and he could make $8 per hour plus tips.

"No thanks," he said, "I make more on the streets."

"Take care of yourself," I said and never saw him again. I never minded helping him out, but I offered a way to build himself back to a productive citizen, and he passed. Me too then.

At this point, Dad was not well. He had lost so much weight he looked like someone had starved him to the point of collapsing. He had met Brendan, which I was so happy about, but inside, I was falling apart. Bob Barratt was the glue that held my family together. Without him, we would splinter, and I was sure of it. For me personally, he was the one source of strength I had, and he was dying. Wouldn't be long now. He was fifty-nine years old and looked like he was eighty-five. I would later find out that I, too, would look eighty-five. Terrible, insidious disease cancer is. Non-Hodgkin's is a form of blood cancer, like leukemia. His immune system was collapsing; fluid had filled his legs and was moving north. He began having breathing problems, so he would sleep in a chair so he wouldn't drown. They couldn't drain the fluid, they said, for fear of causing an infection that would kill him quickly. He was in and out of Hahnemann Hospital in Philadelphia, about ten blocks from my office. At this point, Mom kept harping on me that he was dying, like I didn't notice. I knew it was coming, but I didn't want to think about it too much, as I would begin bawling in front of anyone and everyone. I got a call early on August 1, 2001, and was told to get to the hospital. Dad would be dead that day.

After I ran to Hahnemann, I got up to the ICU. My mother, sister, and brother-in-law were all there as we sat waiting. A doctor came out and sat down. The situation was dire. His blood pressure had dropped suddenly, cutting off blood to his internal organs. This would lead to organ shutdown and death. I asked the doctor, "What exactly is going on in his body?" Just like football, I figured if I knew what the problem was, I could find a way, figure it out. He told me that the human body is an amazing thing. When his blood pressure dropped, his body temporarily shut down his kidneys. Somehow the body knows that it can do without kidneys for a short period of time, so his body was drawing blood to organs that are needed all the time, like his heart, brain, liver, and so forth. The problem was that they were pumping him full of medication to increase his blood pressure, and it stopped declining but was not going high enough for his body to kick-start his kidneys. Even if his body did restart his kidneys, this would happen over and over until the end came. He told my mother directly that he would continue to do what he was doing as long as she asked him to, but ultimately, he could not be saved. I asked Mom if she wanted my opinion and told her to let him go. Nothing could be done.

I fell apart right there in the ICU waiting room. I covered my face and wailed. The rock in my life would no longer be there. I was alone and would be forever. I also thought, *How could anyone deny that there is a God?* Didn't you hear what this man just said? How does the body *know* to shut down certain things to save the life of the whole without God? Amazing. When people fall into freezing water, the body will draw blood from the extremities to heat up internal organs. The problem, of course, is you can't swim anymore, and you drown. But God is incredible in His creation. Now, I had to figure out why my prayers were either ignored or not heard at all. I was angry. They told us Dad's passing would take about five hours after they stopped the medication. I ran back to the office for an hour or so and let the chain of command know that my dad was dying and that I would be out of the office for a while.

I had been writing and rewriting his eulogy for the last three months. How do you sum up an entire life in ten minutes? Especially a man whom I thought I could not live without and had been such a good father? Well, I had to. I don't remember all of what I said, but I will share what I do remember.

Dad loved football, and therefore, I did. He loved to bet on games too. About six months before his death, we were at another funeral, waiting in line to pay our respects. I remember standing there wondering what heaven was like, so I asked him. "Dad, what do you do? What do you do in heaven?" Dad said, "You bet on football games, but in heaven, you always win."

The crowd gathered at the high school knew him very well and howled in laughter.

Another memory just hit me. Dad realized that his kids were different than he was, and I don't think he cared a bit. I think he liked that my sister, brother, and I were all so different from him. I think Dad admired that I was a dreamer; I wanted to play pro football or be a senator someday. And even though Dad was not someone famous or a powerful politician, I think it's safe to say that dad lived his dream; he was a husband, a father, a coach, and an athletic director. And in that capacity, in this small community of Glassboro, dad was famous. Dad would always say not to worry, that things work themselves out, they always do. But I can't help to think that my little boy will never really know that Dad was not only the best father I ever knew; Dad was the best man I ever knew. So, Dad, I'll try. But for me, the sun will never shine as bright, the grass will never be as green, and the laughter will never be as loud as when you were here. I love you, Dad.

Now, I unraveled quickly. My drinking increased and was drunk almost nightly. I experienced confusion, mourning, and a feeling of being alone for the first time. I had no sense of direction; I was angry at God for putting me through this. When you're a drunk, being self-centered comes naturally. PTSD, drinking to mask the symptoms, and now this. I continued to work at Janney in Philadelphia, and I was doing everything I could to just focus on making enough money to take that burden off my mind. I went into work on September 11, 2001, and got there at 7:30 a.m. Around 8:00 a.m., my assistant mentioned that one of the towers had been hit by a plane. He must have lost a rudder or an elevator on his plane or something; visibility was perfect so that couldn't be it. I shrugged it off as almost everyone did, until the next plane hit the other tower. I mentioned to my assistant that I "think I'm retired now. The market is going to get crushed." Fairly selfish comment, looking back. We were under attack; I couldn't believe it. I found the nearest television in the office and watched the buildings burn. I was so naive at the time; I thought the sprinklers would put the fire out and we could start from there. Of course, the sprinklers were ripped out like everything else. The pictures on the TV were from a great distance, so we didn't see people jumping or falling from the buildings. I mentioned that some Middle Eastern country was about to turn into a glass parking lot. I had to explain to a coworker that when a nuclear bomb detonates over sand, the sand is melted into glass. *What am I doing here? Are we next? I'm in downtown Philadelphia for goodness' sake; I'm out of here.*

*****

The train to Jersey was completely packed by people fleeing the city. I have to say, that day the streets were packed as I walked to the train, and not a word was uttered by anyone. On the train itself, cell service was overloaded and shot. Calling anyone was a nonstarter. Women cried on the standing-room-only train; people kept trying their phones to reach loved ones. Of course, I was saddened, but I was angry too. Did someone really just pick a fight with the United States of America? Someone was going to meet the working end of all of our might, I hoped. When I got home, I put a tape in the VCR.

That's videocassette recorder for those less fortunate to know what they are. I began recording this monumental day. I also realized that two of my friends, one of them Dennis Boyle who I introduced you to in the first chapter, guy with flaming red hair and frog legs? He worked in New York as did another friend, Bob McGinty. Bob was an offensive tackle on the team who worked harder than anyone I ever met. He was there too. I got hold of both of them, talked briefly to make sure they were okay, and let them go to call their families.

Oh man, what an awful day. It wasn't until later in the week that footage was released showing Americans jump to their deaths. Empty skies were eerie, not a plane up there. Things were going to change from here on out. In the course of a month, my father passed away, and America was attacked. I needed a plan now; being a broker just wouldn't do it anymore. I started networking. I'm not sure exactly how it came to be, but I talked to a teammate from college, Grear Wolf. Grear had been working for Aventis Pharmaceuticals since college, and I asked if there was anything open that he knew of. He said he would make some calls. In the meantime, it didn't make much sense to keep traveling to Philadelphia anymore, so I resigned. I washed cars for a friend who owned a detailing shop with the hopes of catching on with Aventis.

By this time, my friend John was good enough to allow me to work forty hours washing cars for a dealership. I did, however, begin drinking at work. Then I needed to drink at night since now I couldn't sleep without it. I had been having terrible night terrors around this time, all involving being attacked in some way. At this point, Marcy and I were trying for a second child but were forced to sleep separately. I was getting violent in my sleep. One night, I thought a man was in my room with a rifle pointed at me; I dove down the stairs and woke up at the bottom. I punched a hole in the wall thinking I was defending my family from an intruder. I choked my wife; that can't happen again. I was flipping mattresses and screaming and fighting, all in my sleep. Marcy slept with Brendan downstairs in a different room for safety reasons. It also led to a lack of connection that, in part anyway, started us down the wrong road. It was all my fault, though. Marcy worked hard and was a great mother. She ran the household through all of this. For me, I kept drinking more to keep my sleeping behavior in check.

*****

Grear Wolf introduced me to Steve Wilkinson, and we met at a hotel for an interview. I gave him stories of my military time, as well as my experience in the market. Steve, as a marine himself, understood the military language and was also the kind of guy who wanted to check off his tasks and get to the next one. He had me interview with two other managers and then the regional manager. Waiting for an answer was crippling. I knew the end of the year was coming, and I would probably not start until January, if at all. I knew I was good with people, knew how to identify what makes a person tick and relate to them. I also knew that this job came with a competitive salary along with sales bonuses. I had to wait.

After what seemed like a lifetime, Steve gave me the thumbs-up. *Now, I'll be happy*, I thought. I was on the way to making almost twice of what I was used to. Marcy and I were both excited. All I could think of was paying down our considerable debt. By this time, we had $30,000 in credit cards alone, an incredible figure. That had to change. I began working, training on the medications I was responsible for. I also had to introduce myself to the offices I would be visiting in my territory. That is what I started. I went to each office and learned about their procedures and office protocol. During this time, I would introduce myself as Ron Barratt, not a pharmaceutical salesman. From my experience, people generally don't like salesman. Their opinion, I think, is that we are all Mike Lindell, the My Pillow guy who is all over the television. Annoying and loud; not the tactic I wanted to use. The best salespeople, in my view, are the ones who sell while not appearing to be selling. Go to them from a collaborative standpoint. Say, "What can I do to help you run this office?" We could always get to the technical, "my drug is better than the competition" stuff later. I would begin with a simple introduction and a handshake and then ask them how business was. Many of these physicians ran their own business and were wearing many hats as a result.

Insurance company payouts weren't increasing, but their overhead responsibilities were: raises, electric, and other things. As a result, I approached them from a business standpoint.

The approach was successful for the time being. I made sure I paid homage to the office managers since they run the place. I also made sure I was quick if I didn't have a full-blown message for the docs on any given day. Generally, office staff really are not fond of pharma reps. They take up the doctor's time and cause them to be late for patients. As a result, with each rep who comes in, the office staff can count on getting off work late. Not a great thing for representatives to do, dominate a doc's time. My territory took off, and scripts were going through for my drug in my territory. My bonus was going to be nice. It turned out that my first bonus was going to be $9,400! Wow, more money than I'd seen to that point. We could pay off smaller cards and go from there. Didn't happen. In fact, I'm not sure what we did with it, but I know our debt didn't budge. New rugs, drapes, you name it, and we got it. I didn't mind fixing the house with painters and roofers or whatever the case was, but we didn't touch the cards. On top of this, Marcy would give me $200 per paycheck. *My allowance? What am I, a child?* This started a huge downfall for me. I resented that she had the gall to pretend that I wasn't there, that my opinion didn't matter. I began learning poker; *then* I'd finally be happy.

In 2003, Chris Moneymaker invested $40 for an online tournament and turned it into $3.5 million or something. Crazy. I just kept thinking that if I could have some sort of autonomy or independence, I would finally be happy and please everyone at the same time. I read book after book on theory and strategy. I bought DVDs of top poker players and studied situational poker. I began playing live and online. I don't know why, but I had a number in mind that would lead to happiness. If I could just pay off our credit card debt, we would have the freedom to live our lives the way that I had envisioned. That didn't happen. Playing online is dangerous and stupid in the sense that so many hands are dealt you can play a month's worth of poker in a week. That in itself seems harmless, but the more you play, the more you can lose without some sort of discipline.

Since I drank the entire time I played, discipline was impossible. I was successful playing live and actually won several tournaments. Poker, like football, was nothing more than pattern recognition and human behavior. People seemed to play the same type of hands with the same amount of betting, and I picked up on these patterns. At this point, I had teamed up with my friend and brother-in-law in a combined agreement if we hit a big number online. We did. My take of this agreement was $5,700. I was ecstatic. I took $4,700 of my cut of the winnings and secretly paid off a credit card. This proved to be trouble.

At a family gathering, I let slip that I paid off a credit card. Marcy waited for us to leave to let me have it regarding my sole decision. That is *our* money, I was told, regardless of the fact that I put a ton of time and effort into learning the game and risking my allowance. Several more times, I was dressed down as a result of not handing over winnings. If I won, she took most of it. If I lost, it was on me. This is possibly the worst deal I've ever heard of. No risk, all reward. I had thrown in the towel at this moment. My drinking increased, and mental decline was at an all-time low. I never felt so useless in my life. I began lagging at work, and my conscience began gnawing at me. I woke up late for work and went home early. I was a failure.

HOMELESS

At this point, around 2005, I was doing poorly. Depression, anxiety, and overall despair is the best way to describe it. By now, I had my son, Brendan, who was five years old and daughter, Kelsey, who was just turning one. I should have had it all, I guess. I had a good job and a growing family. I'm sure my wife knew that I was in trouble; it was difficult to hide. We were sleeping in different rooms at this point because of my night terrors, which were showing no signs of easing. Dreams of intruders kept me on edge each time I closed my eyes. One night I woke up at the bottom of the stairs, thinking that someone was in my room pointing a gun at me. I woke up punching what I thought was a bad guy, only to realize I had punched a hole in the wall. I had flipped my mattress on top of my son when he was younger. It was getting dangerous. Marcy decided a change of scenery would be the answer. The town we lived in did not have their own school district and Brendan was being bused about ten miles away to a town that would take the students in our town. That, coupled with my problems, led her to begin to look for a better home and a better town.

About a mile away, in Stratford, New Jersey, Marcy was looking at a house for us to move in to. It was three bedrooms with a built-in pool. Our home in Hi-Nella was two bedrooms and much smaller. Her thinking was to get me to new surroundings and the kids to a better school district. Of course, the home cost much more than the one we lived in, and I thought we would have trouble affording it. I had spoken to her at length how we didn't have enough equity built into the home we were leaving and that we would have to pay out of pocket at closing. She was unconvinced. A friend of mine who I knew through someone else convinced us that we didn't need any money at closing. Everyone was wrong. We owed almost $5,000 at closing. Between us, we barely had $100 to our names, and it threw me into a rage. I was on the phone with our friend who told us we were going to be fine at closing and screaming at him. That was the first of many cell phones that I would break. Marcy's parents bailed us out, of course, just another way for them to pick through our lives and let us know they were watching. I say "our lives" when I really mean mine. I never felt comfortable around them to begin with; now we would never escape their prying eyes and judgment of me.

By now, I had really begun to notice my mental challenges during the day. This was new to me. I could, somehow, always feel a tightness in my chest with an elevated heart rate and could never seem to catch a deep breath. At this point in my job with the pharmaceutical company, I had let it be known to my boss the troubles I was having. I thought it was just something that I had to deal with and get over. My boss echoed that and suggested I get to work. I had never felt so alone in my life. If we went out for the night, I had to sit with my back to the wall and instinctively knew where the exits were. I looked for bulges on the hips of strangers. There were no solutions; nothing I did or could do would make a difference. Even if there were solutions, I didn't even really understand the problems themselves. My life consisted, by then, of being quiet, bringing home a paycheck and closing my mouth. To make matters worse, my daughter had a strange illness that the doctors couldn't seem to help us with. She was swollen in the belly area all the time and throwing up. They had no suggestions. After an endoscopy, it was revealed that she had a pretty severe case of celiac disease, a sort of food allergy that is actually an autoimmune disorder. To this day, she is on a strict gluten-free diet.

One day, behind the wheel at work, I had a panic attack. I had to pull over to avoid an accident. That was it. I couldn't do this anymore. I called my boss and quit on the spot. I knew I would have to explain it to Marcy, but I didn't have a choice, in my mind. At this point, we had trouble brewing, but for some reason, I was confident that I could find a job that would not include so much stress, and I would be fine. I still didn't realize the source of all of this. I began seeing a psychiatrist in neighboring Marlton, New Jersey, with the hopes of getting an understanding and maybe even a solution to all the problems I was having. From my time as a pharmaceutical representative, I realized that, like anything else, there are good and bad doctors. I thought I had a good one. I had never been so over-medicated in my life, to the point of not being able to function. I was on two antipsychotics and several benzothiazines. Mush mouth. My sleeping issue was solved, I guess, but living was impossible. Financially, we ran into trouble as well. I emptied my 401(k), and we lived off that for a while. As a guy with a chronic anxiety disorder, I can also sense anxiety in others, and it always seems to make mine worse. Marcy was growing increasingly distressed, and I could not handle it. It completely compounded my own issues.

My wife and I barely spoke anymore, and that was the most emotional torture I could imagine. Here I thought ending my job as the source of stress would get me back to "normal," and it was only replaced with a silent partner. She snuck around on weekends, preparing to do what she was going to do. She bought a car and asked for a divorce. I was crushed. This was all I had left. My father was gone, and my relationships with the rest of the family were just as acquaintances. Any friends that I may have had at the time all knew I was in trouble, and they scattered to the wind. Alone, no family, no money, nothing. I tried to reason with her. Maybe we could just separate for a while, I said. She agreed, as long as I was not in the house. Although I never laid a hand on her, I guess the screaming from time to time left a mark on her, and she was "afraid" of me. I started living in my car.

As a guy with a sleeping problem to begin with, you can imagine how hard it was for me to sleep in my car. Anyone could look in the windows or try to break into the car. I might have had $50 on me, so of course, I bought a case of the cheapest beer I could find and a bottle of vodka. I also had the dozen medications I was supposed to take on the front seat. I thought if I could just make it through the next two weeks, give Marcy a break, I could somehow miraculously win her back. Being in my car was not a good idea. I know what many thought at the time; just go live with someone. Okay, right, what is your address, and I'll be over in twenty minutes. I was like a lepper; no one wanted to deal with me. The nights began to torture me.

The first problem I had was there was nowhere to go. Police routinely roust anyone from their sleep, check to see if they are a fugitive or something, search their cars, harass them. I feared that. I remember the first night. I was in a parking lot of the local mall, and I thought about praying. *How do I pray? What do I say? Will I be heard? What will happen next?* I gave it a shot and prayed for forgiveness. *Our heavenly Father, please forgive me. I am a horrible man. I have hurt everyone that I love. I am weak and stupid and cannot figure out what is wrong with me. No one will ever love me again. Please, Lord, just forgive me. Amen.* I had completely disrupted my wife's life. I had probably damaged my kids psyche as far as I knew. My prayer was short. I swallowed far more pills than prescribed and had a giant mouth full of vodka to drift off.

I woke up the next morning and thought I could go home for the day while Marcy was at work and watch some television. Then, before she got home, I would just get out of the house and move on so she could have some space. I pulled into my driveway and tried the door. The locks were changed! I almost collapsed. We had agreed that she could have some time off; there was hope. That hope was now dashed. I have been given up on, abandoned. I don't think I'd ever felt that low in my life. I was unwanted, discarded. There was no saving me. I thought of the prayer I had said. *Why can't God just reach down and fix me? Why can't He put me back together? Where is He?*

For weeks I was in my car. I had found a dive bar with a parking lot that was almost pitch-black after hours. I figured the cops would just think that someone couldn't drive that night and had gotten a ride home or something. It worked. I was unbothered for the next two months or so. I remember it was summer and sweltering hot. As a result, I had to constantly run the air conditioner with the windows up to stay cool and keep the bugs out of the car. The only thing I had to my name were some clothes, always alcohol, and my laptop. I would plug the laptop into my car at night to watch *Seinfeld* DVDs to keep my idle mind from telling me how awful I was all the time. It worked, but if I couldn't run the car, the battery would die. Gasoline was a problem. Running the car on idle all night would drain the gas tank. Sometimes, I had to shut it off regardless of the insects and suck it up.

One night I actually was in danger of running out of gas, so I drove to my house that I was locked out of and knocked. Marcy handed me $5 and closed the door, and I could hear the locks being secured. I cried my eyes out. I remember thinking that my prayers were either ignored or not heard at all as I sobbed, getting back in my car to get $5 in gas. That night I drank heavily, as usual. I watched *Seinfeld* until I couldn't keep my eyes open anymore and passed out. While sleeping, I heard someone trying to get into my car. I hit the roof! He had seen the light from the laptop shining, didn't think anyone was sleeping, and tried to break in. I kicked the door open and began to chase him. There was a wooded area right in front of my car, and he tried to escape there. I began to chase him, but once in the woods, I realized I didn't have shoes on, and my feet were feeling the effects of fallen branches. I stopped chasing. I remember the rage that I was in. I actually thought, *If I can only catch this guy, I am going to kill him.* Lucky for me, I didn't have shoes.

Over the course of the next ten weeks or so, summer turned to fall. I didn't have a cell phone on me, and the only thing I had was a pay phone at the same Burger King that I would use the bathroom to clean up in. I did not shower, by the way, if you were wondering. Yes, week upon week without a shower. I was vile. Anyway, the only number I had was the business phone number of a family friend from across the street in Glassboro, New Jersey. I would call and check in almost every day. Thinking back, I don't have any recollection of the actual topics of conversation, but I do remember knowing that I had *someone* to talk to at the time. I called Gordon probably three times a day. What I do remember is that mentally, I was even unhealthier than I was before. My anxiety, which was most likely exacerbated by the excessive alcohol, was far worse than at any time.

One thing I would like to inject here which is a bit off topic is coincidence. There are not coincidences if you look back at your life and the hard or the good times. Do you really think all of that happened by chance? How did you get out of the hard time you were in? Was it luck? With the ability to look back and zero ability to look forward, the conversations I had with my friend were not a coincidence at all. Give me a second and I will explain.

One conversation I can recall with Gordon was a decision I had made to rejoin the military. I wanted to go into the army as a Calvary Scout and get in a fight I could make sense of. I remember saying goodbye and figuring that I would be killed in combat somewhere in Iraq or Afghanistan, and I would regain the honor that I had lost through weakness and stupidity. Cav Scouts have one crazy job in the army. They are a very small unit that has an armored personnel carrier, and they are armed to the teeth with heavy weapons. The problem with that job is they are a small force used as recon units. If they get into a firefight, help is miles away. That's if I remember it right. Anyway, I went as far as talking to a recruiter. Of course, he wanted me. They have a job to do too. The problem was I was mentally and physically unwell. I had gained so much weight from poor diet and taking these crazy pills. I don't think I could have run fifty yards. I also thought about losing the ability to see my kids again. My daughter was barely old enough to know who I was. I had second thoughts.

As the months went by, my despair grew enormously. One night, in the same parking lot, I had a thought. I wanted to confess. The next day, I went into my local parish and asked if I could confess to a priest. The woman at a desk told me that they only take confessions on specific days, and this was not one of them. I was surprised. Why wouldn't she notice that I was clearly homeless? I was a sloppy mess, dirty, and smelled. I had tears on my cheeks. She told me to drive to a neighboring town and try there. I did.

See, now I was determined. This was going to happen. Of course, I was scared to death since I only confessed once as an eight-year-old. I didn't care. I drove the eight miles or so to the neighboring church and walked in. A woman was sitting there as before, and I asked about confession. As she began to tell me I was out of luck, the priest came out of his office, looked at me, and informed me that confession had been cancelled that night and to try somewhere else! Once again, *look at me!* I turned and walked out, this time sobbing. I got in my car and headed back to the parish my kids were brought up in.

I knocked on the door sternly. Again. As my anger began to grow and I was tempted to slam on the door, it opened. An older gentleman in civilian clothes stood there. I said, "I need to confess right now. I know I have been told that you do not hold confession tonight, but I don't care if I have to drive to Pittsburgh to do it. Please, can you point me in the right direction?" He invited me in.

I sat down. I had no idea what to say. I even had to ask, "Do I say, forgive me, Father, for I have sinned?" He nodded in the affirmative, and I began. I described my situation. I shared every sin I could think of. It took forty minutes, if I had to guess. I couldn't keep my composure. I kept crying. "I betrayed my wife. I abused alcohol. I did drugs for a time. I ruined my entire family. I crushed my wife. I yelled and said awful things. Now, I am on the streets, but my wife is now uncertain where they will live. What have I done, Father? Please forgive me!"

He thought for a second and agreed with me. I did betray my wife; I did jeopardize my family's future. I betrayed her with alcohol and mistreating my body, losing my job. He was harsh, but loving, and I sensed that. Then he began the true message. "All is not lost. You are right to come here and confess (I'm paraphrasing), but you are forgiven by the blood of Jesus Christ. He will take this burden off your heart because He loves you."

"Where has He been, Father? I have prayed for months, and nothing has happened."

"You're here, aren't you? He sent you here." Then he told me that when I go out to my car, I would feel a complete lifting of weight off my shoulders. I would cry very hard because the Spirit would be there to redeem me. The next day I would begin a new life. When I got to my car, he was right. The burden I was carrying was lifted. I felt a kind presence. I wept. Coincidence?

With a renewed sense of purpose, I began looking for a job, any job. I stumbled on to a privately owned pizza shop and began as a driver. At least I had a few dollars in my pocket and could maybe begin a way back. But back to what? I wasn't sure, but progress, however small, is progress. After a while delivering pizza and still living in my favorite, dark parking lot, winter was coming. This was going to be difficult. I ended up talking to my friend Chug, who had given me my first job at fifteen years old. He was having his house renovated, so he didn't live there at the time. But I could crash on his couch if I had to. I took him up on it since it was far better than the car. At this point, I couldn't drive to deliver pizza, so I took a job with a friend from home who owned an auto detailing shop. I washed cars and would drive from time to time to pick up a delivery for the dealership.

There were some dark times while I was there. I was still drinking far too much, I was still way overmedicated, and I was in a new place all over again. Acute anxiety is a very short-term reaction that your body has to an actual threat, such as a dog chasing you. Chronic anxiety, however, is a long-term fear of a *perceived* threat that actually doesn't exist. All of us experience anxiety from time to time. How am I going to pay the rent this month? My boss sent me a strange email, what does he mean? Am I going to be fired? Is my girlfriend going to break up with me? These are all small examples of anxiety that we all have. Chronic anxiety is a whole other monster. My experience with chronic anxiety that has plagued me for over twenty years is a real mystery to most who have never heard of it or knew someone going through it. It is difficult to grasp for many and even harder to explain. Why are you clinching your fist? Why are your hands opening and closing constantly? What is that audible grunt that you seem to have? I have learned to consistently lie about it and never enjoy doing it. This is the main reason why PTSD causes isolation, and that causes problems in itself.

On a daily basis, I have some level of anxiety. Most days it is tolerable, say a 5 out of 10. When it creeps up to a 7 or 8, I am in trouble. See, the higher the level gets, the less successful I become at simple things, like thinking rationally. There is a never-ending feeling of having to run for my life, but there is nothing threatening me. I *know* this, but my brain doesn't care. The part of the brain responsible for "fight or flight," called the amygdala, is in overdrive. I know I have gotten offtrack here, so just bear with me because I find this fascinating. The amygdala is a cluster of cells on each side of our brains. Now, here is the kicker; the amygdala kicks in the fight-or-flight response *without any input or initiative* from us. It naturally pumps stress hormones into our blood stream to get the heck away from the threat, *or* attack. We have zero control over what this sucker does to us. Rightly so, I guess. If our Creator left it up to us, we would think for far too long, trying to decide what to do as the lion closes in on us for a free meal. The crazy thing about the amygdala is that it is in our frontal lobes, which are responsible for rational thinking, reasoning, decision-making, and planning. The amygdala "hijacks" the entire area, and all of those things I just listed are overpowered. So in essence, my brain is in a constant tug-of-war. Are there drugs to help? Of course, but any medication should be carefully considered. Our bodies are a gift from God, and He is a genius in His creation. Our bodies react well to man-made medications for a while. Then our bodies get used to them, and the drug efficacy diminishes. We need more. So there is a balancing act that has to be carefully monitored by medical professionals.

So when I was living on Chug's couch, I had a horrible time sleeping despite the medications or the alcohol. That made me up the doses. I began seeing shadows just out of my eyesight. Then they would disappear. I was going mad, I thought. Then, when I began seeing a pattern, another possibility occurred to me. Almost on a nightly basis, I would eject myself off the couch in a frenzy, thinking someone was there to kill me. I also noticed that most nights, it was *exactly* 3:00 a.m. Not 2:59, exactly 3:00. Coincidence? What is the significance of this? Well, it is generally believed that Jesus Christ died at exactly 3:00 p.m. In the war over souls, evil presents itself at 3:00 a.m. to mock the Holy Trinity. Keep in mind that I am not a theologian, a pastor or priest, or some kind of expert on the Bible. At the time, however, I didn't care about that. I was convinced that I was being tormented because although I was not a churchgoer, I didn't read the Bible, or surround myself with other Christians, I was under attack. What I believe is that the prince of darkness wanted to ensure that I would not grow closer to Christ. I was praying regularly at the time. Evil wanted to get me back to where I was. Look, I was still a mess, of course. But I was growing closer to a solution, and that solution is Jesus. A battle had begun. One night, once again at

3:00 a.m., I felt a poke in my chest. This was not imagined. I burst off the couch and ran through a banister that protected the stairwell. I cut my right foot to the point that it looked like hamburger, fell down the stairs, picked myself up, and ran out the door. I really had no knowledge of anything, what it was I was running from, or any other details. I was standing on the sidewalk when I finally came to clarity of mind. I looked down and realized I was bleeding badly. Now I was worried that I had ruined my friend Chug's banister and would bleed on his rugs. What I should have been worried about was that the devil threw me down the stairs and tried to kill me. After all of this time, doesn't the devil know he has no power over Christ? He has no hope of winning!

I believed in our Lord with my heart. I knew that this perfect world couldn't just have happened by a bunch of rocks, dust, and gases could have come together at the perfect distance from the sun to create life. I did not believe that we were once fish, made it up the chain of command to chimpanzees, to Cro-Magnon, to where we are now. I truly believed that this was all impossible. How is it that the Earth spins and tilts at perfect intervals to make it possible to grow crops and feed us almost everywhere except the poles? No, something far higher than man has done this. Look at the animal kingdom and how beautiful it is. There is foliage, grasslands, berries, and other fruits to feed the grazers. Some animals eat grass, which feed predators. Nature is a *perfect* balance. Did man make the trees? I am leaning toward the negative. So if nature and the Earth itself are perfect, what is perfect? God is perfect, that's what. I was growing closer to God, and the forces of evil thought they had a say in this. Attacks kept coming. I have heard people talk about the "big bang." Yeah, it was big and instant. God spoke, and the earth was created. Sounds like a bang to me.

One night, I was sitting outside of my friend Chug's house when my sister Lynda called me. She said, "I'm so sorry to hear that you are getting divorced." Even though I wasn't sure what the outcome would be, I still held out hope that I could prove that I was a good man and win my family back. The air completely came out of my lungs; I almost fainted. When I caught my breath, I was angry.

How could anyone give up on me? I am a strong, talented man! I can always come back. I don't care what the obstacles are! My anger grew. I put the car in drive and began driving back to my home in Stratford, New Jersey. On my way, my brother Bryan called me. By then I had a cell phone. I was so angry; I took it out on my brother. We were not exactly yelling at each other, but I wasn't going to be stopped. I was going to kill myself right in front of my wife as a form of revenge. Evil had a grip on me. I remember I told my brother, "I'll see you on the other side," and hung up. I parked in front of my house, swallowed about one hundred pills and slugged down about three beers. It wouldn't be long. After about ten minutes, I walked in the house with the intention of writing a goodbye note. As I started writing, I noticed that Marcy was on the phone and speaking in a sort of code that indicated to me that she didn't want me to know who she was talking to. Before I knew it, two cops walked in. Ah, now I know who she was talking to. The two policemen were incredibly gracious, polite, and professional. I believe their first question was, "Hey, buddy, what's going on? Come on, man, come with us." I complied and off to the hospital I went. Evil was still trying to win, and I was lost. I had one foot in the water and one foot on land. I was not completely committed to the Lord. It was a battle over good and evil, and I was the puppet on the strings. Unfortunately for the devil, he didn't realize that once committed to the Lord, he has no chance. He was doing everything he could do to make sure that didn't happen.

COLLEGEVILLE, PA

In 2008 and 2009, I had been living with a friend who was kind enough to take me in. He was one of my best friends in high school. I rarely laughed harder with anyone else. He is a great guy and was raising two boys on his own. He was a hardworking, dedicated father who realized we both had a need. He was laid off from his construction job, so he needed financial help. I needed a home. He took me in. The problem was he was an addict too. He had developed rheumatoid arthritis at an early age. The medications he was on had worked just fine for years, but when we got a bit older, it grew worse. Rheumatoid arthritis is different from osteoarthritis. Osteo is just wear and tear, something we all will experience if we are lucky enough to make it to an advanced age. Rheumatoid is the body's immune system falsely believing that the body itself is the enemy. The immune system attacks joints, and over time, he needed a hip replacement. After surgery, he was prescribed opioids to deal with the pain. That lead to addiction, and now another addict joined him in his home.

Our addictions never seemed to conflict, so I was relatively safe there. By this time, I was pumping gas at a local Wawa. For those not in New Jersey, yes, it is the last state in the country that has workers pump gas instead of the driver. And a Wawa is a convenience store that has its roots in New Jersey as an iron foundry. The word *wawa* is the Native American name for the Canada goose, hence the logo. Then it changed to a dairy store in Pennsylvania in 1902 or something. It's the best convenience store in the country, in my view, and other chains are copying their path. Now, they are up and down the east coast only with a heavy presence in Florida, New Jersey, and Delaware. Although I was *only* a gas attendant, I started believing in myself. Coincidences do not exist just in case you are missing the overall message here. Ha. I took pride in showing up every time, on time and ready to go. I thought at some point I would be an executive at the company. I was making $8.25 an hour, but that didn't matter. I always thought, and still mention it to my kids, that I don't care what they do as long as they do it well. I got this idea from Marv Leavy, the former longtime coach for the Buffalo Bills. When he was inducted in the football hall of fame, he told a story of his father's reaction when he told him he wanted to coach football. His father had wanted him to become a lawyer as long as he could remember. When the time came that Marv Leavy had to make a decision, he called his father to tell him with reservation since he didn't know what his father's reaction would be. He told his father, and there was a long pause, then his father said, "Be a good one." I have taken that gem with me ever since. Does it matter what we do? We all want to make money and live comfortably, of course. I tend to think that whatever we do, we have engaged in a contract with our employer. That employer gave us a chance to prove our worth; be a good one.

When I was pumping gas, I realized that there was a group of guys who came in almost every morning to fill up. They all wore the same green shirts. After a while, I got curious and asked the driver who they were and what they did. He told me they worked for a lawn care company and that they go door-to-door to sell fertilizer and weed control. I was curious and asked what the pay was. At the time, I believe it was in the $14 range, plus commission. Hmm, sales; $6 an hour plus commission. I ended up getting an interview, and off I went to this national lawn care company. I excelled at it almost immediately. As a former salesman and a people person, I took into account who we were and what the purpose was for us being there. We were invaders basically. Almost everyone hates having anyone knock on their door unannounced. It was not like when I was a kid. When someone knocked on the door, everyone jumped for joy and ran to the door to see how lucky we were to have visitors and see who it was. Now, people mute the TV and dive under tables like a foreign army is there to arrest us.

With that in mind, I would instinctively back up by about ten feet to let whoever opened the door that I was not there to attack, simply to introduce myself. During the day, it was mostly women home with young children, so I had to disarm them. Aside from backing up, I always made sure I smiled. I would then say something to the effect of "Hi, I'm Ron with ——, I just wanted to let you know that we are in the area introducing ourselves to good folks like yourself. We are offering free lawn care estimates to take care of weeds and get a healthy lawn. Would you like if I just took a walk around and looked around to get a better idea of how we might be able to help you?" I would guess that maybe 20 percent of homes where I made contact would ask for a free estimate. After that, I would first start with the price. Salesmen always make the mistake of trying to jam features and benefits to the customer before they give a price. The mistake they make is that the person in front of them completely tunes them out until they get a price. I started with the price and then would say something like, "Now, what do you get for that price? Well, for starters you would get…" I did well, and I was happy. I earned a promotion to commercial manager at a branch in Pennsylvania. It meant a gas card, higher pay, and a chance of making a decent living beyond the seasonal job I had in New Jersey. I had overcome all my demons and was successful. I didn't need the Lord anymore. Uh-oh, right? No coincidences.

*****

I was still drinking excessively. I thought, because of my night-mares and night terrors, that alcohol was the only solution. One morning, I got in my car and started the hour drive to Pennsylvania. Something was wrong, but I couldn't figure out what it was. I thought it had to do with something regarding my blood pressure and checked my pulse on my neck. I couldn't feel one. I would feel nothing for about four seconds and then, *boom*, a big reaction on my hand. I felt weak and not as alert as I usually was. I imagined that it was because of a hangover or something. I never really experienced hangovers in the traditional sense. Never had headaches or nausea. I had gotten used to feeling sluggish since alcohol causes dysfunctional sleep patterns. In fact, if you look at excessive alcohol more closely, you'll realize that sleeping from alcohol is much like being under general anesthesia. It's not healthy. Anyway, feeling weak was a new symptom of something, so I got a cup of coffee from Dunkin' Donuts, and off to work I went. While on the Blue Route in Pennsylvania, I looked down, and realized I was driving forty-five miles per hour in a sixty-five-miles-per-hour zone. Something was wrong; I had to get to a hospital.

I decided to drive to Paoli Hospital, which was forty minutes away. It was a hospital I knew, and it had a great reputation for competence. I went to the front desk at the emergency room and told the receptionist that I didn't feel right and thought there was something wrong with my blood pressure. The ER nurse hooked me up to an EKG machine and turned white. He looked at the readout and asked me if I had ever had a heart attack. I hadn't. He rushed to get help, and I was later admitted for atrial fibrillation. From my understanding, A-fib, as it is referred to, is a condition where the upper chambers of your heart are fluttering or beating way out of control. The fluttering causes the lower chambers to slow because not enough blood is there for them to pump blood throughout the body. Once they fill to a proper rate, they finally pump the blood to where it needs to go. That was the boom I had felt. A-fib is a serious condition primarily because as the upper chambers don't pump properly, the blood pools idle and can cause blood clots. Strokes are much more possible. It had to be dealt with.

After two days, the medication was not proving to be effective in getting my heart out of this dangerous condition. They were forced to use paddles, if I remember correctly, to zap my heart back into rhythm. Keep in mind, that at this time, I was approximately 240 pounds packed on my five-foot-eight frame. I was completely unhealthy in every way, physically and spiritually. I was told by the doctors that excessive alcohol use was the cause. Of course, I had no understanding of this but was informed that I was "pickling" my heart. I was given medication and released from the hospital. My life was attacked once again by the evil in my heart, but the Lord continued calling me by saving my life once again. There were no coincidences. All I needed to do was surrender my life to Jesus. I was still blind, however, and stuck in the belief of just believing in Him, and that's it. One foot in, one foot out does not work. I was still blind.

The commercial manager at this national lawn care company was completely misleading. I did not manage people, just accounts. They did this because then, because I was on salary, they could mandate one hundred hours a week if they chose, and I had no recourse. Brilliant, right? Slap a manager label on us so they can pound us into the ground. I worked sixty hours per week every week of the year. Even so, I still had the belief that you put your best foot forward and do the very best that you can. I pored over my accounts and tried to put a value on them. What accounts put meat on the table? Which ones deserve my complete and total attention? Which are problem accounts? I had come across an account that was a consulting company, looked it over, decided it was a solid account that was on autopilot.

Months later, I got a call at my desk in the morning from this consulting company that there was a problem with the property. Keep in mind that I did not consider myself someone who just fertilize properties and put down weed control. I considered myself a property manager. I called everyone back. I gave each property the same attention and professionalism regardless of how big or small. The woman who owned the property was telling me that she was not getting the results she expected. I got in my company truck and headed to Collegeville, Pennsylvania. When I pulled up, I realized it was a residential home with about an acre. I walked to the door and rang the bell. I stepped back as usual, but I also always took my glasses off so the customer could see my eyes. In my opinion, people have the right to see who they are dealing with, and the eyes are the gateway to the soul. They will instantly know by looking me in the eye that I am professional and want only customer satisfaction. When she opened the door, I removed my sunglasses and put them on top of my hat. She had just gotten home from the gym and was dressed in that attire. The look on her face was priceless. She almost covered up in embarrassment, blushed, and said hello. I instantly knew we would get along. I told her who I was and the reason for being there.

As we walked around the house, she let me know that the property was brown, and there were weeds popping up. Most customers think that fertilizer and weed control are perfect solutions to everything. It was the middle of summer and blazing hot for weeks with no rain. Although I used to tell everyone that the only thing I can't control is rain and that in a drought they need to water, they rarely ever did. I got more calls about brown properties than you could imagine. I could tell instantly that she was interested in me, and not just as a property manager. My confidence swelled. When I was younger, I had much more confidence to approach women. Now, in my forties, my self-esteem was lacking. She brought life into me. I was interested too. After spending about an hour with her, I asked her if she would like to get a drink sometime. She agreed. Yes!

About four days later, I realized that I had concert tickets to the Goo Goo Dolls in Atlantic City. I really enjoyed their music and looked forward to seeing them. I had a problem, though. Who in their right mind would agree to go down to Atlantic City for a concert for their first date knowing that we would have to get a hotel for the night? She agreed. It was the best date I ever had. The Goo Goo Dolls was such a great show. There were young and old dancing and enjoying their wonderful music. We danced and had a great time. I had a future with this woman. On our way back, we decided to stop at a convenience store for cold drinks. She went in while I waited in the car. I have to admit that my sense of humor is strange at times, but I have always been told that I am funny. I had an idea. Not only was I waiting in the car; I was driving *her* car! I decided, as a joke, to pull down the street as if I had left her there and stolen her car. I waited anxiously about fifty yards down the street. I couldn't wait to see her reaction. She finally came out of the store, looked around for the car, and burst into laughter! Oh, she's a keeper!

I began staying at her place while still paying rent in New Jersey. We had gotten together almost every night and enjoyed our company. After a month, I suggested I move in instead of commuting an hour-plus all the time. She was hesitant but agreed after a few days.

I moved in for what would be the next eight years. As is my pattern, things went swimmingly for a while, and then the bottom dropped out. Everyone gets sick of me over time. Wow, I have said that maybe a thousand times in my life. The problem is it happens to be true. Even as you read this, I am confident that you will ask me to leave after a while. You might even get sick of reading this and throw it in the garbage. I wouldn't be surprised. I'm much too high energy and always seem to fall time and time again. The constant anxiety from my past haunts me every day, even as I type. I always seem to try to overcome my internal lack of love for myself by making others love me instead. I am funny and project a confident demeanor, and I have a wonderful ability to communicate. I have been hiding behind that for twenty-five years now. Unfortunately, every day the sun goes down. As it does, my anxiety creeps higher and higher with every passing moment. When the adrenaline gets to dangerous levels, I become almost paranoid, very defensive. I check windows when the ice drops in the freezer. I am always on guard at night, which makes for sporadic sleep at best. I am constantly exhausted. Let's get back to Collegeville.

Almost nightly we would spend hours drinking and talking at her kitchen table. I enjoyed this so much because not only is she a wonderful woman and I enjoyed her company, I also had a distraction from the idle mind that torments me. Our conversations were incredible. It was the happiest I had been in years. We would also go out at night constantly. We would go to the local restaurant/bar and enjoy everyone there. We became regulars, and everyone loved us. I was ecstatic. One night, as we walked in, I noticed there were about five people near the front door. It was a perfect time for my twisted sense of humor. When we got close enough for them to hear me, I said to my partner, "Is this the first time you ever ordered a male prostitute?" Absolutely hilarious. The gasps I heard made us laugh for hours. The clock was ticking, however, when the time would come that I would wear out my welcome. It was just a matter of time. Until then, I would enjoy where I was.

*****

Her uncle Bill and his wife would visit once per year. Bill is a Vietnam veteran. He and his wife were wonderful company. The first night I met them both, we sat at the kitchen table for hours, and I was blown away from our conversation. I needed to know in much detail what it was like being in Vietnam. I asked question after question. How did you get ammo? What did it look like? What was base camp like? How about the men you served with? Who was an outstanding leader and who wasn't? My partner asked me to go out on the porch for a moment. When we got there, she said, "What are you doing? We are not supposed to talk about Vietnam." I replied that if I were to offend him, or he was not in approval of my questions, I was sure he would let me know that he was not interested in talking about it. When I mentioned that to Bill, he told me that he was actually appreciative that someone took an interest in his experience. He mentioned that his family never asked one question and thought they never appreciated what he had gone through.

During their two-week stay, they came and went. They visited family, but each night, we found ourselves back at the kitchen table and later out for dinner. We got along very well, and he showed the same level of interest in my military experience. Shared appreciation and respect for life. Also, during their stay, I could hear him shouting at night. The next morning, I mentioned it to him. He replied that I did too. I knew I had nightmares and night terrors but had no idea that I screamed in my sleep. We began talking about the Veterans Administration. He was still waiting for a response to his appeal to get 100 percent disability rating. We began talking about what that all meant and what to expect. For years, I had been intimidated to approach the VA. I didn't know how, where to go, and who to speak to. I also had reservations because I thought myself unworthy. For my little encounter with a guy in a dark room? No, there are far more deserving men and women who were in actual combat. If I accepted help from the VA, then I thought I would be displacing someone else who deserved it. He asked to speak to me alone. My partner and Bill's wife left the room. Bill and I sat there. I thought I was in some kind of trouble.

As a side note, every veteran I have spoken to in detail about their service, if the conversation led to it, said none of us did enough. We all could have done more. Someone else is far better than I am. If we did four years of service to our country, we should have done more. We didn't sacrifice enough. While Bill and I spoke about this, he assured me that I am just as deserving as any other veteran with problems related to our service. I nodded over and over and tried to change the subject in a respectful manner. He saw that I was being a bit dismissive, stopped, and said, "If you don't go to the VA for help, you're a f——ing idiot." I promised to follow his lead and his orders. In the meantime, however, he had spoken to me about his yearly reunions. The next one was scheduled to be in Washington, D.C. in a month or so.

I spoke to my partner and asked if she would be interested in going to Washington for his reunion. She said she would ask permission. I am drawn to others who have sacrificed for others. These men certainly fit that bill. I wanted to be there among others who sacrificed far more than I did. I wanted to show them support and be among them as a guest. Our request was enthusiastically approved. Bill's family followed suit. He was thrilled that his brothers and sisters would finally be there to learn about his dedicated service. We went, and it was an incredible story. I met a bunch of fine men and their families. Tommy Franks, retired general, was also a member of the 5th battalion of the 60th and 9th Infantry Division in Vietnam along with all the other men there. It was a great experience. Uncle Bill introduced me to so many heroes, but if you'll permit me, I'd like to pause talking about my experience and share Uncle Bill's experience.

As you can imagine, war is not a pleasant place to be. There is always a chance for lighter stories, and I'll share one with you here. Over the years, I have heard this story more than once, and it is funny. Communications were primitive in the time of Vietnam, and Uncle Bill was the radioman for his platoon. It was an early form of a cell phone, I would imagine. He was the one with the suitcase-sized box on his back when he was there. The commander during any firefight would circle above in a helicopter to manage strategy and where to focus the forces on the ground to defeat the enemy. In one firefight in the Mekong Delta, Bill was in a rice paddy during the engagement. In rice paddies, as it was told to me, there is water separated by berms of soil. The berms ran row after row. In the waters of Vietnam were uncountable amounts of bloodsucking leeches. During the fight, if my memory is accurate, Bill lay down on one of the berms as the fight went on. The commander above saw him tugging at his pants with his rifle at his side. The commander spoke directly to Bill since he carried the radio. "What are you doing lying down? Get back in the fight!"

Bill replied, "Sir, I have a leech on my penis! I have to get it off!!"

The commander called down again and said, "You can deal with that later! Get back in the fight!"

Hilariously, Bill replied, "Sir, I'm eighteen years old! My penis is the most important thing I have!"

Time after time, every time I hear this story, it is incredibly funny. Other stories are not so pleasant, and they are much less frequently shared.

Another veteran I would like to share is Bill's dear friend, Lee Alley. I don't have permission to share his detailed stories, but his book, *Back from War*, is a recommended read. You can also see some interviews on YouTube if you choose. The purpose of me bringing him up are a few quotes. One is, "The enemy owns the night." He mentions that when he and others came home from Vietnam, they either became workaholics or alcoholics because the enemy never leaves, especially at night. Lee Alley is Wyoming's most decorated veteran—distinguished Service Cross, Silver Star, Bronze Star, two Purple Hearts, and Combat Infantry Badge (CIB) among others.

> As a Vietnam veteran, I too have felt the sting of rejection. I too, have felt the slap across the face of a nation, who disrespected my service. How in God's name, can you tell a soldier whose arms have held a bleeding and dying comrade, yours is not a noble war? (Lee Alley, PBS Wyoming)

The point is, PTSD doesn't discriminate and doesn't care how brave or strong you are. It doesn't care about the political correctness of a war; it is a never-ending battle within. It doesn't only come from war, either. It is simply trauma; it can happen to anyone. When I speak to veterans, many of those I have helped get their benefits, I always ask the same question, "Okay, now what do we do?" That means that regardless of the situation, many of which are bad news or experiences, what do we do about it? This reminds me of a story from *The Chosen*, a series on the gospels that was an incredible teaching tool when I was new to Christ. One scene, after Jesus had banished seven demons from Mary Magdalene, she once again fell prey to darkness. She fell down in her faith despite actually walking and talking with God in human form. Keep in mind this is from *The Chosen*, which tried very much to stay accurate to the gospels but admittedly had to fill in some blank areas. I'm not sure which one this is. But when she returned to Jesus in complete shame, she shares with Him that He redeemed her and she threw it all away. Jesus responds by saying, "Did you think you would never struggle or sin again?" Darkness and evil are always probing the fence line, looking for weakness in all of us. It is the "what do we do now" and how we respond to that is the key here. Jesus has offered all of us His hand; it is up to us to take it.

*****

At this point in my relationship, my partner and I were coming to a point where we were at odds a lot. I had enough of the lawn care thing. My territory had gone from tenth to third during my tenure, but my regional manager, who never sold a thing in his life, was a bully and a completely negative man. During a conference call on a Friday, he called me out by name in front of all my coworkers. I was enraged. The constant, "we need more sales" thing got so old I could barely breathe. *Of course*, we need more sales. Did he think I wasn't aware of that? What leadership book did you read this gem from? I took the weekend and quit on Monday. Now, my girlfriend had suggested that I take a month off from work altogether. I gladly agreed. For a month, I played PlayStation and lounged around. This bothered her tremendously. What did she think I was going to do, put an addition on the house? I would try to do dishes, only to be told that I didn't load the dishwasher properly. When they're done, are they clean? Then what difference does it make how the dishes are loaded? Wash was another one. I could go on and on, but the main thing that was decided can be summed up by a conversation we had. She told me that she hated the PlayStation, that I should be doing yard work or some other chores. I told her that the PlayStation is a box of plastic; you can't hate a box of plastic. You hate the fact that I enjoy it, which means you hate me. I always enjoy when I meet a new woman. She is so excited to meet me, she knows what I do, and who I am. When the honeymoon time is finished, however, they somehow think I am going to morph into some whole different person. Well, despite the fact that she was and still is a wonderful woman, I was about to wear out my welcome. I could feel it.

The stress of knowing my time was limited caused my normally high anxiety to climb to incredible heights. I would have a nightmare in the middle of the night, wake up, and go to the vodka bottle for a mouthful to speed up the calming down period. It was starting to get bad. I was told to leave one morning; she gave me twenty-four hours. I moved into what we referred to as The Chateau.

The Chateau was a "rent by the week" establishment for the dregs of society, which I had become a card-carrying member of. It was fairly disgusting run-down boarding home to the tune of $140 per week. I fit right in with the drug addicts and everyone else. I was experiencing a new low here. At this point, I worked for a wire and cable company in Collegeville, and although they are incredibly successful, I think this may be the worst company I ever worked for. First of all, in my interview, I was told I was an "old dog" and "we don't hire old dogs." I guess they looked for young kids they could bully into submission. They may have been the most negative place I've seen in my time. Every Monday there was a meeting for the folks just building up their business, only to be told how awful everyone was. Yeah, this wasn't exactly the best fit for a guy with anger management issues and PTSD. The one saving grace, though, was that most of the time, we were cold-calling potential customers, something I excel at. They could see that I was good on the phone and that saved me for a while. The other processes were stupid, with ridiculous details in how the order would ship and other things. I was having a hard time dealing with all the details that were involved. That, and the fact that I had nowhere to go, made my anxiety go wildly out of control. By then, at lunch, I would have to go back to the Chateau and swig a couple mouthful of vodka just to keep from blowing up on someone. In the afternoon, I would cruise, killing it on the phone. I couldn't keep this up, though, and I knew it. I knew that people would smell it, so I avoided everyone. This wasn't going to last. Then I would be homeless again, which scared me into drinking even more. Like a hamster on a wheel, I was sprinting but getting nowhere.

My girlfriend and I were still in contact, and once again, we enjoyed our time together. This is a very common occurrence, just to be completely honest. I am taken very well in small increments. I always ruin everything in the long run. God help me. Anyway, one weekend morning, I woke up and was now into the morning drinking thing. Not good. I was so depressed and upset. By now alcohol was having such a negative impact on my mind that I was now pickling my brain. I got into an argument on the phone with her, and once again, I decided to throw in the towel. I swigged whatever booze I had and dialed some kind of hotline for mentally diseased individuals. I told them I was going to go to the Walt Whitman Bridge and jump but didn't want to drive because I had been drinking. Ha! Yeah, you can either call me responsible or completely crazy. I think it was both at the time. They questioned me about who I was, where I was, and so forth. I don't know, but either I told them I had PTSD, or they knew. I'm not sure. But by this time, I had spent considerable time at the VA, had gotten an official diagnosis, and had gotten shot down twice for a disability rating. They asked me if I had any weapons on me. I said, "Sure, I have tanks, rockets, aircraft, and bazookas all crammed into my tiny room." You would think that they would know I was joking, but in the end, they couldn't make any assumptions. I got off the phone and calmed down. I thought it was over. I went downstairs to have a cigarette when I was passed on the stairs by four PA State Troopers. When I was downstairs, they followed me and asked if I was Ronald Barratt. I affirmed that I was. There were five of them in front of me and had me backed up to the wall. A female trooper was very kind and professional. She did all she could to disarm the situation. She said they were just going to take me to get help. My mind was racing, and I was in combat mode, surrounded by five troopers and being told to turn around and get on my knees. I'm not getting on my knees for anyone. I raised my jacket to show I was unarmed and assured them I was fine. At this point, a trooper to my left, some young Rambo type, said, "So this is the Iraq PTSD p——y, huh?" Oh, this did not go over well. I replied, "What did you just f——ing say?" I tore off my jacket and lunged for him. I didn't get far, since I was tased three times by the other troopers. Once cuffed, they rolled me over when Rambo began hitting me in the face with a closed fist over and over. My left eye closed pretty quickly. *What a hero this guy is*, I thought. Of course, they whisked him off the scene, and none of the others would give me his name. A sergeant who had showed up thanked me for my service. With a battered face, I told him to not let Rambo at any other scene. Better keep an eye on this guy, Sarge.

Once again off to a loony bin, only this time strapped to a gurney. I had to get an MRI on my brain, of course, just to determine if Rambo had caused a brain bleed. The loony bin is even more exaggerated than *One Flew Over the Cuckoo's Nest*, believe me. Schizophrenics and worse. After five days, I was released. Jackie's mom picked me up and lectured me, rightfully so, on the way back to the Chateau. Probably not the time for it, but she might not have gotten another opportunity. After heading back to the wire and cable company with a monster black eye, I knew I could not continue. I lasted maybe another week when I was let go. *Praise the Lord*, I thought. Now, I had a problem, though. I could no longer pay for the Chateau. One night, my last night there, I was asleep when I felt something on my chest. I grabbed it with my thumb and finger and squeezed. Something shot out of it. I turned on the light and realized it was a bedbug. Oh no, uh-uh, not for me. I gathered up my clothes for burning and limped back to Jackie with my tail between my legs.

TREATMENT

Things at this point were not going well. I had been in counseling at the VA for a while now and even had taken an anger management course by this time. I was delivering pizza just to have a job so that no one would bombard me with negativity or harass me at any level. It was a mindless job that put a few dollars in my pocket without any threats to my fragile psyche. I was with my girlfriend, and we shared many friends. Although I had no embarrassment or problem with "just" delivering pizza, our friends were wealthy. They seemed to take me in as an equal, but that was not the case. I began to notice early on, but I always give people the benefit of the doubt. We all socialized on a regular basis. I also had a friend next door, Aaron, who I still call friend. He is a good man, and we shared experiences and still do. His girlfriend whom he lived with, however, had deep-rooted emotional problems that did nothing to help my own. Just like anything else, the more you get to know someone, the more you tend to pick out traits that you find undesirable. Our friendships began to suffer. I always had the ability to look forward but seemed to lose it at this point. It was 2016, I believe. I was looked down on. I left the pizza empire I was building and went back to lawn care with a regional, family-owned place.

As usual, I believed the grass would be greener, but with every job I have had, there is one common denominator, me. At first, I enjoyed being there. I was back knocking on doors and interacting with people, which is my wheelhouse. One of the sticking points was that, as a regional company, we did not have the name recognition that the national company had. With the green company, I would knock on the door, and they would see my shirt and know exactly what I was there for. With this company, I had to go into depth as to the reason for my knocking. This greatly reduced the number of prospects and sales. It was much more difficult. They also had much higher prices, which put us at a disadvantage. Lawn care is run the same everywhere. The cost is based on the size of the property. Once agreed on, the technicians would come and treat the lawn. As a salesman, who is expected to bring in business on a daily basis, I would have to cut costs to the customer to stay competitive. Unfortunately, this was a conflict with the technician since they were required to treat a certain dollar amount of lawns every day. We routinely butted heads. "You totally underpriced that property! Why should I waste my time doing it?" I would always reply, "So you can keep a job." Sales and production, a constant argument.

It didn't take long for me to realize that my sales manager was under great stress and not handling it well. I tried to lighten the load on him by training new hires for him. One winter I actually wrote a training handbook that the new hires could read, study, and understand the sales process. It had illustrations of weeds, trees, and shrubs. It also added role-play type of conversations to give the guys a better feel for how conversations should go. The sales manager, under pressure, started losing his cool on a regular basis. He had hired some incompetent guy from Bath Fitters, his last job. This guy was so bad I am not sure if he is competent enough to have any job, much less be on the phone or knock doors. Anyway, new guy was driving the manager crazy, and shouting started. My anxiety went through the roof. Not only did I have the stress of having to work in a seasonal job again and bring in sales daily, but now there is shouting at a guy that he hired. Was he surprised? When we worked inside because of weather, I would go to lunch and have a half pint of alcohol to alleviate the constant stress this guy caused me. *Great, now I'm drinking at work! Not good.* I also started to envision throwing this guy off the roof of the building. I would have to shake myself out of it. I was coming unglued quickly. I did not work long for this company.

One day, I got up and had tremendous pain in my stomach. It was also accompanied with diarrhea. Wonderful, huh? I thought whatever it was it would work itself out and I would be fine. After two weeks, the pain grew more intense, and I was having a hard time walking. I needed to see someone. I went to the Philadelphia VA emergency room. They asked for urine, which after all the drinking I had done over the years, looked like coffee. After a CAT scan, I was told I had diverticulitis, a semi-common infection in my lower intestine. I was also told that they had gotten a good look at my liver, and it did not look right. I brushed that off, of course. I was given antibiotics for the intestinal infection and referred to the gastroenterology department. After an MRI, it was revealed that I had three grape-sized tumors on my liver. Uh-oh.

I spoke to the head of the GI department, Dr. Dave Kaplan, and he explained that they needed to conduct a procedure where they go through my groin, up into my liver, and put a chicklet-sized chemotherapy on the tumors themselves. I thought, *Hey, no problem. Whatever it takes.* On the morning of the procedure, Jackie and I made our way to the Philly VA. I was brought into a room for the procedure, which consisted of a metal "bed," camera equipment, and other machines I couldn't identify. During this procedure, they give you an anesthetic that doesn't quite put you out. It leaves you in a state of in-between. They still needed me to be responsive to directives, like hold my breath. The metal table was painful for me to lay on. My back bothered me for a while as a result of years of football, I guess. As the procedure went on much longer than I expected, my back hurt more and more. I started to squirm and writhe in pain. I was told repeatedly to stop moving. They told me that they were going through an artery in my hip, and if I kept moving so much, I could bleed out if the artery ruptured. The procedure ended, but my back pain did not. They had me pumped up with morphine at this point but did little to give me relief from the pain. I kept sitting up and trying to stretch my back. They told me to knock it off, that the artery had only a glue-like substance on it, and once again, it could rupture my artery. They threatened to tie me down. I told them they might have to. I was in agony!

After maybe two weeks, I was told that the tumors were neither growing or shrinking. That indicated that it was not cancer, but they would have to confirm with a biopsy. Super. That procedure went far better than the first, and the results came in negative. I was in the clear, I guess. Dr. Kaplan told me to hold on. After MRIs, he told me I had cirrhosis and that the liver was dying. I thought he was being hyperbolic, of course. He told me that 40 percent of my liver was basically dead. Cirrhosis is like emphysema in the lungs. Once there, it cannot be improved by any means. I thanked him and left. I didn't drink for three weeks, which was a first in my experience over the course of many years. I googled percentage of liver function. Of course, it said anyone can live many years with 50 percent of liver function. I took that opportunity to drink again to "reward myself" for being abstinent for three weeks. Great idea, Ron. I also began praying daily for the Lord to help me stop drinking.

When bad habits become normal, they are less likely to dissolve. I had to stop and do it right then and there. I would go weeks without booze, and then anxiety would hit me for some reason. The racing heartbeat, inability to catch my breath, clammy skin, shaking. If I can figure out a reason for the reaction, it is so much easier to deal with than when I have no clue as to what is causing it. There have been countless times that I pace back and forth, trying to figure out what is causing it. It almost always gets worse when I have no clue. Then the feeling of "what should I be doing that I am not doing?" is awful. The feeling is so uncomfortable that I will do almost anything to make it go away. Since I had only been seeing a psychiatrist and psychologists for maybe a year at this point, they would not prescribe anything for it. This is one of my beefs with the VA. I don't know how many times I have asked for short-term relief, not a three-month supply but maybe five days and was told "Nope. Try deep breathing." I just got done telling you I can hardly breathe at all! "Go for a walk." Hey, dummy, if I can't breathe, how am I supposed to walk? They do not prescribe any antianxiety meds, ever. That makes sense. Combat veterans come back with a brain disorder that can't shut the adrenaline valve down, and you tell them to go watch the movie *Beaches* or something. Wonderful policy. So let me see, what other choice do I have here? Hmm. Ah! Alcohol!

By 2017 I could barely stand to go to work anymore. Not only did my manager complain if I had doctors' appointments; I was being toyed with as to the number of sales I was generating. It was winter!

To make matters worse, I was taking Chantix to stop smoking. The medication completely worked to keep me from smoking. The problem, however, was it caused whacked-out dreams, which I didn't need help with. But it also caused fits of anger, which to me were also normal. On February 4, 2018, the Philadelphia Eagles, my hometown team, were playing the Patriots in the Super Bowl. I drank, of course, and the mixture of Chantix and alcohol had a devastating effect on me. I was an emotional wreck. I was angry and couldn't figure out why. There was nothing to direct my anger toward. On top of that, I had a bad cold; triple threat. My girlfriend had been away with friends. When she called and heard my voice, she knew I was in trouble. She sent an uncle to the house to check on me, and I blew up behind the door. I yelled at him to go away and leave me alone. Jackie told me she was on the way home.

I panicked. I did not want a confrontation in my state of mind, but I was drunk. I got behind the wheel without shoes, my wallet, or phone and left the house. Instead of simply driving to a parking lot and sleeping it off, I drove while blacked out and came aware when I was on Villanova's campus. I tried a parking garage. No good, needed a key card. I turned around and went into a loop. Instead of staying right, I went left when I realized that there was a cop directing traffic for construction work. I stopped and waved him over.

"Sir, I have no business being behind the wheel. I don't want to hurt anyone. Can you help me?"

He directed me to back into a loading dock. I asked him politely not to beat me, as I had Rambo on my mind from a couple years earlier. I told him I was a veteran with PTSD and to take it easy on me. I had turned myself in, and I was asking for help. He called a veteran police officer to come talk to me. He was empathetic and professional. I blew into the tube, and off to the hospital we went. I did not know the level of alcohol in my system, but none of that mattered. I watched the Eagles beat the Patriots on the TV in the room I was in.

During the night, there was a terrible ice storm; roads were covered. Since I didn't have a phone and we don't remember anyone's phone number anymore, I was in a bind. I did know Jackie's number, but in an effort at tough love, she would not come pick me up or give me anyone else's phone number. The only other number I could recall was my mother's. I called, and she said she might be able to pick me up. She's in her late seventies and was probably scared to drive. Understandable. She gave me my sister's number. She came to pick me up as the hospital was urging me to leave as soon as possible. With all the rock salt everywhere, walking in socks was painful. We went to the police station to get my car back. I needed my driver's license to do it, so we had to drive back to Collegeville to get my wallet and then drive back. I needed to focus on the PTSD and all the ugly things that come with it. I decided to check myself into treatment.

The next week, I was staying in a hotel when in the morning I decided I had enough of this reckless life I was living. I called my high school friend Mark, who is also a veteran and the founder of pawshealingheroes.org, and asked him how to do it. He referred me to a marine veteran who had been there, and I spoke to him on the phone. He suggested that they would not admit me unless I was drunk. What? *That's crazy*, I thought. I followed orders and drank on the way. By the time I got there, I thought I was a bit buzzed, but that was it. When they gave me a breathalyzer, the results were a 0.18 BAC. No way, I said. I checked in for the next thirty days. Classes were about the effects of drugs and alcohol on your body, groups, one-on-one treatment, and nightly meetings to watch a video or hear a guest speaker. I settled in, managed medication with the help of the staff, and cruised through it. I was worried about what caused the alcohol, however, and that weighed on me.

When I reached the end of my month's stay there, I spoke to my staff sponsor about a PTSD program. These types of programs always include a substance abuse overtone since they go hand in hand. He suggested a facility in the Hudson, New York region. A few miles from West Point, this was going to be a challenging program. One thing I was not crazy about was the fact that they take your phone and put it in storage. I had written many numbers down on a small pad, so I thought I would be okay. That turned out to be difficult. There was only one phone to make outgoing calls only, and there was a time limit, but no one stuck to it. It turned out to be days without talking to my kids or others, and then when I would call, they didn't recognize the number, so they didn't pick up. The other thing that turned out to be challenging was that they had all of us so drugged up nobody could stay awake in groups or in the lounge area where sleeping was forbidden. We all referred to the psychiatrist as "Dr. Feelgood" since all he did was shove pills down our throats.

The counselors were professional and helpful for the most part, and groups weren't that bad. But some of them tried to act like we were all still in the military, giving ultimatums or talking down to us. I, for one, did not like this at all. It had been over twenty years since I took orders. I had no intention of returning. I would say, "Or else what?" to many of the ultimatums. Didn't they realize we were there voluntarily? We're asking for help, and they are talking to us like we're children misbehaving. The other concern was that there was a young man there who simply didn't like me. Hey, it happens. What can you do? For the most part, I avoided him, but he would seek me out. He had more than just PTSD, or he simply couldn't control himself. I'm not sure, but he didn't like the way I talked, which was surprising since we were all from the Northeast. He tried to correct something I said twice, and I let him. This was in between his meltdowns that the staff seemed clueless how to handle. One day in the lunch line, I said something that he found offensive, and he snapped and yelled at me. Nope, not going for it a third time. I told him never to tell me what to say or what not to say ever again. I asked if he understood and forgot about it.

Now the youngster was upset because I put him in his place. Another one of the guys approached me, and I reiterated that I didn't care what he wanted; I'd speak the way I do. I didn't care if it offended him or not. I said, "Why don't you go down and tell him right now?" He did. Of course, the youngster came back up and asked if he could speak to me. I agreed. I'll give anyone a word with me; no harm in that. When he started to speak, however, he was aggressive, and I shut him down. He did not like that one bit. He put up his hands as if to fight. I stood there and told him to put his hands down before I get my daughter to kick his ass. He didn't like that one bit. He started to lunge at me, which I didn't care about. My adrenaline was going, and I was completely willing to engage. Lucky for him, a couple other guys grabbed him. This was on a Friday.

Staff got together as expected, but I was confident nothing could disrupt my treatment since all I used were words, and that was *after* he showed aggression and the intent to harm me. Monday morning, I went to my usual group and was asked to leave. Oh boy, here we go. I was asked into a meeting where the staff sat there, and the director of the program began to speak. It was clear from the onset that they wanted me to leave, as if I was the problem. Yes, I didn't diffuse the situation, but I didn't believe that was my role there. They did mention that I was "snarky" throughout the program, which made me laugh a little bit. So because I have a wise attitude, does that disqualify me from the program? My arguments didn't get very far. Looking back, I think they realized that the young kid had more mental problems than the rest of us. Since he was black, they didn't want to be seen as just kicking a black kid to the curb. In an effort to be politically correct, they had to let both of us go. My theory anyway. My big concern at the time was, where do I go next? I had a long way to go, and they just pointed to the door. I went back to my room and packed up. My roommate, another older black man who knew me better than anyone, suggested that I contact Senator Pat Toomey from my home state of Pennsylvania. I asked why, and he let me know that Toomey is well known to be a watchdog for veterans since his father was treated poorly as a Korea veteran.

When I got home, the first thing I did was look up Pat Toomey's office. I explained the situation and that my big concern was that the Hudson Valley VA took a combat veteran with severe PTSD and just made me leave. No backup plan, no alternatives. Not even a suggestion. I was starting over. I voiced my opinion to his office and forgot about it. Maybe ten days later, I was copied on his response. He wrote a scathing letter about how they failed me as an individual and that he wanted a personal letter from any staff who acted as a leader or counselor to answer for their actions in writing. I was blown away. I had never even met the man. It was impressive.

At Philadelphia VA, they suggested Bath, New York as my next stop. This was a four-month program, rare, I found out later, and there was total focus on learning what is going on and how to manage the problems that come with the PTSD. After the five-hour trip, I went to check in. Regardless of the reputation of the place, I was nervous. Any change causes anxiety to a guy with chronic anxiety. This program is heavy on responsibility of the veteran there. Not that they don't monitor what is going on; they do. If you skip classes during the day, they won't bother you until it becomes a pattern. For the most part, however, you are on your honor. Like most things, I chose to put what I had into it. These are the experts, not me. Why not simply trust that they know what they're doing? I met some great guys, a couple I still keep in touch with.

Many of the counselors themselves were recovering addicts so they had some skin in the game. There was one obnoxious lady who constantly put the group down and complained about "behavior." I thought she was nuts and did the best to steer clear of her. My problem with this person was that we were all there voluntarily in order to heal and get help doing it. She was completely out of line, in my view, by dressing guys down or ripping into the groups she was there to help. Over the course of the program, it happened way too much for my taste. We had a mandatory group of most of the men there in the auditorium. As you can imagine, guys were chatting while we waited for whatever it was to start. She just stood there observing with a nasty look on her face. I could tell what was coming. She began to speak, and I could feel my heart start racing. My anger grew the longer she went on. After over a minute of being lectured, I yelled out, "WILL YOU JUST GET ON WITH IT ALREADY!" Almost every employee whipped their heads around, and some gasped. Some shouted that I was out of line. *That's it, I'm losing my cool here. Let's get out.* One guy turned and followed me. He was speaking in a disarming tone, so I tried to gather my cool. I told him that she had a habit of marginalizing all of us, that this was a pattern that had been going on, and I'd had enough. I went back to my room.

When I got there, the building monkey saw me return to my room. I knew he saw me but hoped he would have the common sense to simply let it go. He did not and came walking into my room. He ordered me to return to the auditorium.

Not going to happen, pal, now what?

"I can make you go back if you want."

"Yeah, better go get some help."

Silence passed for maybe ten seconds as I waited for some kind of conflict. See, when the adrenaline is pumping, logical thinking is gone as I stated earlier, but your body *wants to act on it.* Here is where the problem lies. It is very hard for me to keep my cool when I am challenged. This is something I pray for daily while I thank the Lord for another day, His grace, and His love. I'm getting better over the years, but I still have to be careful sometimes. Cooler heads prevailed, I explained my frustration with the woman and her antics. He relayed to me that he had heard that many times from other guys and that I could try to relax in my room. It was over.

While the program went on over the next few months, I was in the process of upgrading my disability rating. I had been turned down twice. Then, after hiring a psychologist to write an appeal for me, I was at 50 percent. I was fine with it at the time, but it wasn't enough. I looked back on my work history. I had been a stockbroker when I got out of the navy, and I loved it. I was a natural on the phone since I worked so hard at it. I practiced in a closed room for hours before I had the "pitch" down cold. Then there was the rebuttal book. These are planned responses for excuses people use not to invest in whatever you are selling. Once I had those down, I was a killer on the phone. This was during the Internet rage and the time Amazon launched as an online book seller. Ha! Look what it is today. Then March 10, 2000, came and the bubble burst. It got harder and harder to make any money at all. It was understandable, but this was the first time I felt a strong sense of what anxiety was even though I couldn't figure out what it was. From there, I bounced from job to job over the course of the next fifteen years. I got worse and worse; I just couldn't take it. At this point in my life, I truly figured I would be better off not working at all but needed to be 100 percent.

I had put in an appeal with the VA while I worked at getting better. At the same time, I began praying even more, not knowing if I was heard or not. Looking back, it is obvious I was, but at the time, I was unsure. We went to AA meetings, listened to guest speakers, and *relearned* how to live sober. We also had cognitive behavioral therapy, which is trying to learn to concentrate when emotional and not let the adrenaline control our behavior. At this point, I had really begun to be curious about who Jesus was. Where did He go? Who went with Him? What did He say? How would He handle troubles? Of course, because this is a government-run program; religion has no place and is discouraged. I had a Bible at home with no access. I didn't think about an application for my phone. The store on base did not carry one. The only time I got to read anything was when I had time to go to the library. At this point, I was completely confused by the Bible. I didn't even know at the time that the words of Jesus were in red. I had no idea *how* to read it or where to begin. It would have to wait, aside from my praying.

After maybe three months, I checked my checking account in the morning and realized that I had a large sum of money deposited. Never even considered that my prayers were heard at this point. I went down to the computer room to confirm that 100 percent rating was approved. I wanted to make sure that was the cause of the deposit and not some bank error. It was not a mistake or a coincidence. The Lord did hear me, yet I still didn't realize it.

After I found this out, I also realized that I was eligible for a VA loan for a house. I did not know this. I had used it once with my ex-wife, and I thought that was the end of it. Back then, veterans could only use it once. Now, the law had changed, and you could use it again as long as there are no flipping houses. I called my friend from high school, and he began looking for me. I would have to do this by phone. I also began to worry about the end of my time coming up. I had settled into the program; I had not had a drink for six months at this point. This was the longest streak I had in years. I felt great, comfortable, and normal for the first time in a long time. For the last month of the program, the therapy got intense. We had long bits of homework to do. We had to write essays about our experience and direct our intensity at our addiction as if it were a person. This was tough. There were a lot of incredibly shame-inducing things. I still had to deal with the DUI on the Villanova campus, just to list one. I also was paranoid for the same reason I got worked up when

I got there; I didn't know what to expect. But my friend Chris, the agent looking for a home for me, found one. I did everything by cell phone. At least I had somewhere to go.

Pre-Covid

Not long after I moved in, I went to visit my brother only a town away. He did not look good. He had trouble getting to the door, which I tossed up to maybe drinking too much. My brother was once one of the most dominant wrestlers in college and had won a national championship. Now, he was incredibly skinny and pale. He had always been a heavy marijuana smoker and never saw the reason for it being illegal. I had spoken to him just a bit about his construction job and where it was. He was working at Fort Dix, a military base in New Jersey. I told him that there is no such thing as discretion when it came to the military, and if they caught him, he would lose his job. Well, that's exactly what happened. Now, he was in a major depression. He had filed for unemployment and had been rejected. He told me he was done, that he had had enough. I reminded him of his dominance in wrestling and asked if he had ever gone on to the mat and thought he was going to lose. Nothing seemed to sink in.

About a month after that, my mother called to tell me that Bryan had died, and she needed me to get over there. Apparently, he had a heart attack and hit the floor. His girlfriend said he had been there for about eight hours; she didn't realize he collapsed. Now, we had to wait for the medical examiner and were not allowed in his home. There was also a state trooper outside and would not let us in. They had to ensure there was no foul play. When the medical examiner got there, three hours had passed. He began by asking questions: date of birth, social security number, and so forth. I grew frustrated and interrupted him. I reminded him that my brother had now been lying there for eleven hours and if he didn't go get him off the floor, I would. To me, it was disrespectful to leave anyone, let alone my brother, on the floor when it was now acceptable to go get him. I guess it's a military thing: leave no man behind. But it bothered me. He was laid to rest next to my father in my hometown. I sang at his funeral, as I did for my father, Josh Groban's "To Where You Are." It is a beautiful song, and he has an incredible voice. If you are not familiar with the song, I strongly suggest taking a listen. But in the song, the lyrics "and isn't faith believing all power can't be seen" struck a chord with me, along with the other lyrics. I was ready for the Lord.

Moving into my home in Clayton, New Jersey, was a challenge I was bound to lose. I moved there to be close to my mother in case she needed me. I had boxes everywhere, a couch, a bed, and no TV. I didn't have my service dog yet, was alone, and deathly afraid when the sun started to go down each night. I still do get freaked out when it happens. I could barely sleep because I was on window patrol most nights. The ice machine would make me hit the roof. I had to deal with this and stay sober at the same time. This was going to be an issue. It was summer of 2019, and I was in trouble. I stayed sober for maybe a week and, *bang*, I fell pretty hard. Instead of focusing on emptying boxes one at a time, I went to the liquor store. Instead of working on my house, I was paralyzed by the fact that it wouldn't take care of itself. I believe that this is the time that I began to come under attack from the powers of darkness. I slowly got the house in order but was always interrupted by alcohol once again. I later learned that this is the reason for fellowship at church. A wounded lion will usually leave the pride, isolate, and go off on its own. This makes him vulnerable and weak, a wounded target for predators. The same goes for active Christians. Fellowship is a monster part of my life now. I need to be around positive, focused people in order to stay strong. More on that later. For now, I was chipping away at my house. I began praying for godly help.

At this point, I would stop for weeks at a time, only to have the devil whisper in my ear a suggestion. That's all it was, a suggestion. I would always have these ideas, and the rationalizing would begin. I would sit on my couch, look at the clock, and realize there was only an hour left until the liquor store closed. *You know you can't do it.*

You might as well give up now. Look, you haven't drunk for three weeks. Reward yourself. I would then spring off the couch and off to the store. That would kick in a pattern. Drink for a week straight, stop for two. I was making progress in my mind, but my doctors were still warning me that liver disease is incredibly painful. I would find that out later. I was so scared at night I was beside myself. My dog, Shiloh, was only five months old, and I had two more months to wait while she was trained. She is a Belgian Malinois, and I asked for her specifically. I didn't want a Labrador or a beagle. I wanted something scary enough to dissuade people from approaching me because I also have a problem with crowds. I called the trainer and asked for her early. I had to wait a month.

Waiting for Shiloh was crippling me since I was overwhelmed with fear. I had gone to the trainer and worked with her myself. Veterans have to get acquainted with the dog in order to build a sense of cohesion. They have to know that *that* is the guy it'll take care of. We would work at a Lowe's for a decent amount of room. She was now six months old, and my trainer didn't want to give her to me yet. Aside from sit, down, stay, heel, she was also trained for my sleeping disorder. When I start to act out, she will lie completely on top of me to make sure I don't hurt myself. It's amazing. At the time, however, she was young and raw. It was getting toward the end of 2019, and she finally got it. Belgian Malinois are incredibly smart, athletic, and loyal as they come. The only two issues they have are they shed like I did when I was nineteen years old, and they are so excitable they want to constantly play or work. Other than that, I doubt I will ever get a different breed. Now, she's a seasoned veteran and my best friend; she goes almost everywhere I go.

I was really starting to settle in and gain some confidence. Shiloh followed me everywhere, slept with me wherever that was, and was on watch all night. Every once in a while, I would hear something, and my heart rate would skyrocket. I would look at her, and she would be sound asleep. *Great*, I thought, *I guess I have to go check it out. I have to go interrupt the guy breaking in and take a machete to the chest!* Of course, if there was a situation like that, I'm sure she would be there and deal with an unlucky intruder. But this was my fear of sleeping taking over my brain instead of having common sense. During the end of 2019, they began mentioning some respiratory disease that began in China. I didn't pay much attention. Then the news began sharing how contagious it was. I'm guessing, but maybe by February, it was spreading more rapidly. By the next week or so, lockdowns hit the country. The one thing I can say is that the dog was a lifesaver, and that pawshealingheroes.org was a major player in making my life easier. It is a nonprofit that saves the dogs from any shelter, saves the dogs, and then has them trained to save the veterans.

Now, I was in a much better place. I had my Shiloh to help reduce the anxiety that I carried on a nightly basis. You would think this would be easy, but it was not. Anxiety, as I have stated, is relentless, and rational decisions go out the window quickly. I was approaching a challenge that I had no chance of winning. I was weak and vulnerable.

THE LORD

In March of 2020, lockdowns went into effect. Scary time. There was nowhere to go and nothing to do. In New Jersey, the only stores open were liquor stores, which for me was a bad situation. I guess they didn't want people dying of withdrawal, I don't know. But I took full advantage of them being open. I would grab a wine bottle-sized bottle of vodka and head home. I would watch YouTube videos and sing along. I would be happy for a short period of time. Then, after waking from a drunken stupor, I would do it again. I would watch the news and see if there was any sign of returning back to normal. There were no such signs. I have to admit, although I had been drinking for years, and in the short term I enjoyed myself, I did not feel very good. I hated waking up to a dark sky and then go through anxiety all over, but I did. This went on for months; there was no relief in sight. To make matters worse, I had a habit of calling people whom I had a history with to share in the glory days. This only opened me up to sounding drunk on the phone, which I was. I stopped from time to time and would go two or three weeks without a drop. Then the suggestion would call me back. Darkness is on the case at all times, despite your best intentions. I remember praying constantly for the Lord to rid me of the burden of these suggestions.

After praying, I would feel strong. The Lord was with me. Then the suggestion would overtake me, and I would lose once again. The suggestions would be in the form of a thought. *You have gone three weeks without a drink. Reward yourself. You know you can't resist…* And off I would be. COVID lasted forever, I thought. I had no escape. I prayed to our heavenly Father for His help to make me stop drinking over and over. Nothing seemed to help. Until the next day.

It was Christmastime, and I was flat broke. The shame of not being able to give my kids a gift wore me out. One morning, I was putting together a drone for my son, Brendan, when my life changed.

Keep in mind that I was ashamed of myself because I had no money for gifts. But I did have a drone that I wanted to gift to my son. I was kneeling in front of a lounge chair trying to put it together. The screws were tiny, barely big enough to hold them between your finger and thumb. I dropped it. *Oh man, now what do I do?* I looked down and tried to find it; nothing. I went and got a large piece of tape; nothing. Then I got a magnet; I was determined to find this thing. I didn't want my son to see a piece of scotch tape around the battery pack. Nothing. I stayed on my knees and prayed out loud: "My heavenly Father, I know this is ridiculous, but I pray for you to help me find this tiny screw. Please help me, oh, Lord. I need to know that You are real and are with me." I gave up and stood up. I felt something in my slipper that I was wearing. It was the screw! To me, this was impossible since I dropped it straight down while my feet were behind me. I knew it was the Lord. I stood up and looked around. I didn't know what I expected to see, but I did it anyway. I held my breath. The sounds of the traffic stopped; the birds stopped singing. I remember standing up and saying, "Lord, are you here right now?"

To collect myself, I went over to the couch and sat down. I was still in a state of confusion. I kept trying to hold my breath to hear something. I decided to drop to my knees and pray. "Oh, Heavenly Father, I pray to You to declare that I am a sinner. I have denied You for far too long. I now have no doubt that You have loved me and looked after me for all of these years. I want You to know that I will follow You until the end of my days, and I will always love You." At this moment, I felt a small wind come into me, and I had a visualization of Jesus on the cross. It was a slow visual of His feet and ascended up to His agonizing face. It was incredibly powerful and nothing more than an affirmation that I was the Lord's cherished son. I wept as a result of this experience. I had never felt such powerful love in my life. I was saved. As usual, I wanted to know who He was, what He said, and who He was with. I remembered the Bible my friend had given to me. It had been on a side table for far too long. I randomly opened it up to 2 Corinthians 5:17, which reads, "Therefore, if anyone is in Christ, he is a new creation; the old has gone, the new has come!"

Coincidence? I couldn't believe that I had just read that. This was the Spirit speaking directly to me and letting me know that the Lord had just claimed my heart. I had to share this. I wanted to go to church. I knew Jeff Crispin, who was three years ahead of me in school, was a pastor, but I had no idea how to contact him. I also knew that his nephew Joe, is a godly man, and he is the head basketball coach of Rowan University in Glassboro, New Jersey. I looked him up online and contacted him.

Keep in mind that this is during COVID-19; nothing was opened. People didn't go to work, the gym, go food shopping, nothing. This was unprecedented. A month went by, and then another and another. After three months and knowing my history, I started to think back to a time I might have insulted Joe Crispin. He was the son of my baseball coach, and the most I'd ever said to him was, "Hey, buddy" when he was eight years old and I was eighteen. *Why hasn't he gotten back to me?* I started to get a bit paranoid when he called me back. That Sunday, I went to Joy Fellowship Community Church in Pitman, New Jersey. Four days later, trouble presented itself.

Keep Moving Forward

The night of June 22, 2020, I didn't feel right. I couldn't point to anything specific, just didn't feel all that great. I had been abusing my body for so long; it could have been any number of things, so I put it out of my mind. My stomach started to bloat, noticeably so. After a couple of hours, I noticed that my stomach was distended. Something was wrong. I remember speaking with a doctor two years earlier who asked if I had ever had paracentesis, a draining of the abdomen. *Of course not*, I thought. I decided to get up and look at myself in the mirror. My face was jaundiced; I was in trouble. It was 2:00 a.m. This was going to be the longest night of my life.

The Veterans Administration is both very capable and incredibly inept. I always found it ironic that they work there to serve veterans any and every day; except Veterans Day. Classic. Anyway, I went to the desk at the emergency department and got the usual hand wave; we'll get to you when we get to you. *Okay, nothing is imminent.* When I walked back to the office for blood pressure and other things, the nurse said, "You all yellow!" *Wow, catching on. Yeah, that's why I'm here!* They took me back to a "room" in the emergency department, and I took the usual two-hour time-out while waiting for someone to address the issue facing me. My urine was the color of tea; it really was no secret why I was there. For years, I hated myself. I was too weak to handle the situation that kicked this all off. I was too weak to be a good father and husband. I was too weak to hold a job. Weak. Now here I am. I have finally found the Lord. A burst of energy shoots through me, and I have a challenge to face.

The main ER doctor walked in and asked me if I drank too much. He knew I did; he had seen me before. Knowing the answer and asking the question in an obnoxious way does nothing to help the situation. It's like walking into a man who is dying of lung cancer and saying, "Shouldn't have smoked for so long." Yeah, no kidding. Do you walk up to a guy who gets hit by a bus and remind him to look both ways?

He said, "You know you are going to be dead soon." Couldn't believe my ears.

"Really?" I said. "How long? Two years? Six months?"

He told me he had no idea. I asked him, not too politely, to about-face and get out of my room. I had work to do.

Dr. David Kaplan, head of the gastroenterology department in the Philadelphia VA, and I had some contact. He was there when they thought I had liver cancer. He was there when he counseled me to abstinence. He walked me through each step. In his midforties, if I had to guess, he is a complete professional in every sense of the word. He is kind, stern, and always knows his patient. He instinctively knew how to talk to me. He started out with the basics: through your experiences, your behavior brought you to this point. See? "Your behavior." He didn't fool around. He was smart enough to know that I knew how I got here. This is a classic example of "what now" that I like to share with other veterans. Okay, bad stuff got you to bad stuff, which led you to even more bad stuff. Got it, now what? Dr. Kaplan ran through what was going on in my body and offered the "now what." Okay, he said, you are dying of liver disease. Pow! Like smokers with emphysema, your liver cannot function properly. Without a transplant, you will die, and it troubled him to tell me that. I could tell.

He said, "Ron, you do not want to die of liver disease. It is incredibly painful, and there is nothing we can do to help you with the pain. You are going to face a challenge you never thought you would have to face. I am sorry."

"Well, Doc, I got me here. How do I get me out?"

Dave looked at me and said, "Most people simply get up, shake my hand, and go home."

"What do you mean, they give up?"

"Yes."

"Well, you got the wrong cat for that. What do I need to do?"

Dave gave me about thirty-five different tasks to complete in the next three months. MRIs, EKGs, stress tests, colonoscopy, endoscopy, another MRI. The list was endless. I was determined to finish. He told me this in November of 2020. By January, everything was done, and I was squeamish to get it all on the table. As you read this, please keep in mind that I am trying to hold your attention while also attempting to inspire. But just now, as I type, I had a flashback at how hard it was. I grew weaker; I couldn't eat. I started losing weight at an alarming rate. I was swollen, muscle atrophying. I would like this to be an incredible story of bravery and courage. What it really is, is a story of a competitor that found the love of Jesus at exactly the right time.

The Lord's hand has always been there. Believe it and take it. If you are the kind who chooses to believe that a man can make a tree, well, best of luck to you. None of this is by accident; you are not a coincidence. You are not trivial. The Lord knew your name before you did. He knew where you would be and what you would be doing. Take solace in that. Who else looks after you while also giving you the freedom to choose to turn away? Your parents? Maybe. Even they pray to the God who made us all that you will make good decisions. I will tell you later of a relationship I have with a man who is "this close" to knowing the true power of God's love. Hope. There is always hope. In the meantime, please realize that I am a man who struggles every day. I know God loves me, yet I still struggle. It always makes me wonder when I hear others say, "Lay your anxiety at the feet of the Lord." Of course, I do! I pray so much that the Lord is probably tired of hearing from me at this point. Why can I *not* simply *be*! I have felt the power of God's love, I have seen Jesus on the cross, and I have felt the Spirit come into my body. You would think that my life would be perfect then, would you?

I apologize if my writing bothers you. I skip around, but what I am saying is 100 percent in my heart. My journey was with Jesus, and it still is. I still pray to walk closer to my Lord and be a better man tomorrow. I will never be a pastor, but I will tell the story of Jesus.

During my suffering, at first, I expected nothing less. I expected some pain. I expected some challenges. I never thought that I would have to literally fight for my life. My body began to go away. Body fat eaten away, muscle starting to erode. Yes, this is what death looks like. I had never before experienced so much pain. I could not move. I could not walk or eat. My body was destroying itself. I remember so many times crying out to God to just take me in my sleep. I had enough! But I couldn't, could I?

I had no choice. I could not give up. I had found the Lord for the first time in my life, and quite frankly, I don't give up. Let me just say that I was more than willing to leave this earth, to die and meet my Savior, Jesus Christ. I still am. But I had a score to settle, and if the Lord gave me time to live, well then, I would do anything and everything to bring His message to as many people as I could. On top of that, I cannot, and will not, ever, ever, give up. Hear that again. I will never, ever, not once, ever, give up. As veterans, we hear many things. Crying is acceptable, crawling is acceptable, puking is acceptable, falling is acceptable. Quitting is not. Live it.

The body is a miracle. We are capable of so many things. If dropped in freezing cold water, our bodies will draw blood from our arms and legs to warm the vital organs to keep us alive, even for a short time. My body was dying. Nothing could stop it. I had been seeing Dr. Kaplan for months, simply for upkeep, I would imagine. I could not function. I am not sure how best to describe it. The whole time this was going on, I simply was freezing. If you look up liver disease, you will find that almost half of the patients experience the feeling of freezing to death. I was one. I could not get warm. I would constantly wear sweatshirts and blankets and have the heat on. None of it worked. Of course, during this time, there was a sense of settling in. I adapted. There were times that I felt fine, at least according to me. No one else saw or felt the same. I was dying right in front of my friends who came to visit me, and of course, to those closest to me. This is not a wonderful experience.

By this time, I had a strong relationship with Jeff Crispin, my pastor and friend. He and other pastors would spend time with me and speak about the Lord, as I was to be baptized in February of the coming year. We would watch videos of various books of the Bible. We spoke in detail about Apostle Paul and the suffering he endured. We would play Mercy Me videos, sing along, laugh, and cry. There were two videos that I watched repeatedly: "Say I Won't" and "Almost Home." These songs helped motivate me to endure the pain, give thanks to the Lord, and look forward to my eventual healing. The church community would shovel snow since I could not. They fixed my fence. It's amazing that I had waited all these years to come to the Lord. What a reward!

By 2021, I noticed that my friends wanted to see me. Why I was so naive I couldn't tell you, but about once per month, my friends from the college baseball team would visit. I really looked forward to these visits. Sometimes I felt great and could sit up; other times I simply couldn't do it. I did not realize then, as I do now, that they were saying goodbye and that I had meant something to them at some point. I had made them laugh, or maybe I was just a good guy. Because of my focus on living, I could not admit that I would be dead soon without divine intervention. My dear friends, Ed Yaris and Dennis Machulsky, kept me going on a daily basis with phone calls. Ed also took me to many of my appointments. Wonderful man. Without them, I doubt I'm typing right now. They had their own heartache and their own problems. The last thing I wanted was to interfere with their lives. But you know what? This is flat-out expected. Why is it that we choose to suffer in silence? Why do we isolate? A wounded animal will go off on its own and make itself a target for predators as I have said. Why do we think we are so much different? We are not. This is why we need the church. We need fellowship. We need people who think in the same positive way and look to the Lord for salvation on a daily basis. Anyway, I for one never thought I was going to die. Everyone else did, but I did not.

I remember the feeling of the Lord coming into me. I have never felt a more intense feeling of love come over me ever. I was convinced at that moment that I would survive and live to tell His story. Was I completely convinced? I'd love to say that yes, I was. But, either way, I was going to live or meet Jesus. Win-win situation. In February of 2021, I was toast. The Lord would save me, or I would go on like everyone else who has ever walked the earth. By that time, I had completely engaged my life and focus into the Lord that I had no other interest. Jesus, the one perfect human being who came here specifically for us, for *you*! Why would I focus on anything else?

I remember speaking to my pastors on a regular basis. They didn't say so at the time, but they all thought they would save a soul and pass it on to heaven. They all thought I was not long for this earth. My church in Pitman, New Jersey is a small one. There are not many bells and whistles, just good people all with the same intention. I am not clergy. I am simply a man in trouble, wanting to understand the meaning of true love once and for all. Jesus is love. If anyone wants to simply google His name, do it. Will you find anger? Will you find hatred? No, you will find love. I wanted and still want to know Him. Who am I to understand someone so simple yet complicated? I want *Him*. Wow, that just came out. I hope you feel the same. I was complete in my aspirations to know Jesus; now I just wanted to know peace.

Physically, things had to be decided. I couldn't walk anymore. I could not dress myself. At this point, I was seeing a woman who confuses the word but had me mesmerized. I will speak more about her later, but she is a representation of darkness that attacks especially when we are alone and vulnerable. At this point, the doctors had told me that I really had no chance of a liver transplant. I have A+ blood, one of the most common. By then, it had been recommended that my only chance at living was through a living donor. Okay, great, now what? The only chance I had at a living donor was my son, Brendan. I couldn't possibly do this. Under zero conditions, can I do this? I cannot ask him. Look, I did this, my cross to bear. I'll gladly die to avoid asking my son to save my life. Unfortunately, that was my only choice.

When it became clear that I was definitely not going to survive, I had a choice. I had one choice. I had to ask my son. Do you know the shame I felt knowing that I had to ask my boy, my son, Brendan? I was so ashamed and still am. I did this. I destroyed my body. I *did*. Brendan did not come along with this. I did this. I still can't handle this. I pray that our heavenly Father will heal me. I am not worthy.

My son and my Father, please forgive me. I am weak and can't do this. I am so sorry. Unfortunately, I had a problem. I had to deal with this. I was in so much pain I couldn't even begin to describe it to you. I cried out every night in agony. "Please, my heavenly Father, please take me. I can't take the pain anymore. Please set me free. I want to meet Jesus. I want to be among others who care about Jesus. I can't take this. Please set me free."

You know the thing about dying is that if you are lucky, it will be slow. The one who suffers is ignored, just look. I was dying. People came to visit. I am so ashamed to tell this story because I could not give in. I could not quit. If you want to think that is honorable, knock yourself out. I will never give in. Please understand, however, that I have no fear of death. To me, this is the most fundamental conversation we can have. Who has defeated death? Only one man, Jesus. Are we so prideful and ridiculous that we think we are so wonderful? I am a diminished man; I am a work in progress. Faced with what you have in front of you, how do you do this?

To be honest, I wanted my son to save my life. As a veteran, I thought it was a no-brainer. Let me, for a second, tell you what it is like to be a veteran. I have four friends, that's it. Done. We are simple people; we like horses, a kind conversation, or a movie. We are not complicated until you make it complicated. I do not know a man who will not stand his ground who calls himself veteran. I was dying and had no idea how to approach my son. I couldn't. I am a failure. How could I talk to him about this? Well, I did.

One morning, we were on the way to the University of Pennsylvania. There was an air of rubbish that we couldn't escape. He had to make a decision. Save Dad's life or not. I still can't take typing this. I am going to die. We all are. Who cares? Do you know that my Father was the most important man I could even imagine meeting? Yes, have you ever heard of a man called Jesus? Brendan had mentioned that maybe he would not save my life. I was okay with it. I deserved my fate. A surgeon came in to our room. I had no interest in giving in, but I was more than willing to go home to Jesus.

I was a mess. I was so cold and so weak that I remember the doctor's face. He simply looked at me and, with a nod, knew I was never going to see him again. To be honest, I had enough. I was will-ing to give in. As we sat there, I remember being lost. My son took all of this in. The doctor Point-blank told me that I would not live. He told my son I would never live without his help.

The doctor basically told Brendan that I would die. I was far too sick, and time was against me. Even if I were placed on the transplant list, I had no chance. I am type A+ blood, which is far too common. There were thousands of guys ahead of me, and even those at the top of the list were dying to the tune of approximately three thousand per day. I was so okay with that. I couldn't fix the conversation. I gave in. I had nothing left. When the doctor left, I asked Brendan what he thought. To me, of course, I was biased; it was my life. But since I never once feared death, I wanted a simple answer. He said he wasn't sure. I almost fainted. I thought for a second, and once again, the suggestion was on my right shoulder. See? You're going to die. He left you when you really needed Him. I immediately had this idea to just go home. It was over at this point. Why keep fighting? I thought for a second. *Well, I lived a good life. I have nothing left in the tank. I'll just go home and drink myself to death. After all, why wait? Why go through incredible pain when the outcome is all but certain?* At that moment, I thought again. I said to myself, "Hold on a second. Me, quit? Me, give in? Seriously?" I suddenly felt the same wind simply brush through me. It was the Holy Spirit. I had two experiences with the Lord. He loves me, always has.

I was in no position to make any demands of anyone. I was freezing all the time, dying a very public death, and simply wanted loyalty the way I give it. I don't care if you are in Haiti and call me at 4:00 a.m. Don't even bother to tell me what you're going through; I'll get you. Without a second thought, I'll get you. We can always work through details later and determine what to do next. I couldn't walk. I was in a wheelchair. I had been told all this time about the MELD (Model for End-Stage Liver Disease) score. A normal person's score is 1 or 2. I was at an 18, but real danger only began in the midtwenties. I held steady at 18 for a while. I knew this to be the case. Google is both wonderful and the constant annoyance to doctors. I had googled the disease and learned that I had maybe eighteen months to live. No problem. When a year went by, I got a bit nervous.

When the doctor told my son that I had no chance, I got a bit more anxious. He told Brendan point-blank, either save your dad's life or don't. After a good cry, Brendan walked me back to our car. I caught my foot, couldn't recover, and fell flat on my face. I cried like a baby; I was so embarrassed and ashamed but could not get up. I lay there, in the parking garage, wondering how I got here. How did this happen? How did I make this happen? I couldn't even put my hands out to protect myself when I fell. I was that weak. We got home, and Brendan offered his help. He said he would help me. I cried my eyes out. He had agreed to help me. My son offered to help me. I was still going every week for the draining of my stomach. This was terrible. I had been there and back over and over.

LORD'S WILL BE DONE

During this time, I had gotten so used to being cold and weak. I began speaking with a churchgoer from Florida, a woman who's name I will not disclose. I loved our conversations; we spoke about the Lord for hours. I knew her family when we were kids. She is older than me, and we just hit it off. Everyone else in my life was screaming about red flags. I didn't see it. I visited in Florida, but I couldn't keep it up. Walking that far in airports was almost impossible. I looked so old security just assumed I was over seventy-five years old. On my first visit to Florida, I got to her house, so excited to see her. There were fifteen stairs to climb, but I made it. We went into her apartment. I sat on the couch and her on a chair. She put something on the television and didn't say a word for two hours. I tried making conversation. Nothing. The next day, I was scheduled to meet a dear friend about another two hours south. I was completely confused about our lack of conversation. We had spoken on the phone for hours like kids and now, nothing. I think she said three words until she said she had to go to bed. She had the day off the next day, and I asked if she wanted to meet a close friend. She said she would think about it. I almost left in the middle of the night but thought if I fell down the stairs, I would never get up. In the morning, I asked again if she would go meet my friend. She said no but asked if I would come back after seeing him.

I got to my friend Mike's house, and we spoke for hours. It was time for me to leave, and he asked me to stay. I am very hesitant to sleep anywhere I am not comfortable since I have such a difficult time sleeping in the first place. What if I tackle a lamp or scream? No, I could not stay. He asked me if I was going to see my "godly" woman again. I told him I didn't think so. She didn't say a word to me, I told him. There was something about her that was not right. When I left, she texted me and asked if I was coming back. No, I told her, I was driving straight through, back to New Jersey. She was shocked, which I didn't understand. I told her she never spoke to me, and I felt awkward. She made some excuse about not feeling well or something. I didn't believe her, of course, but what did it matter now?

When I got home, we regained our conversations, and I was back to really enjoying our talks. I fell in love over the phone. Crazy. All the warning signs. I guess I was desperate for love in case I left this earth. We visited each other a few more times, and I began to really love this Florida woman. I began sending her money to help her with her monthly bills. She worked very hard and did not make much. I thought it was a nice thing to do. Yes, big mistake, and I would later really learn what a mistake it was. She would fly to New Jersey, and we would talk about the Lord and enjoy our company. I was really in love with her. She met my mother and my sister. When we were alone, I got more advice on what a big mistake it was being with her. What kind of woman enters a relationship with a dying man? The kind who is waiting for that to happen, I suppose. I ignored it; I loved her. Many of my friends also had the same warning. Feeding her money was like feeding stray cats. Once there, they never leave. I was also advised that she wanted survivor benefits in the chance I died. "What do I care," I would respond. "I'll be dead. She can have half of my lifetime VA benefits." I also realized that soon I would not be able to care for myself at all. I was finding it almost impossible to shower or dress myself. I was going to ask her to marry me.

I bought an engagement ring and about five things from the Dollar Store. I would mix the ring inside ridiculous things. I had been telling her about my dream to drive an RV across our great country, so I got a small RV toy. I got a few other things and put it in a bag. I flew to Florida, which would be one of my last. I was becoming far too weak. I was so excited about her reaction. By now, I looked so bad they mistook me for a man twenty-five years older. I didn't mind. I got through security without taking my shoes off. How funny is that? I got to her house and presented the bag. She chose most of the trinkets I had purchased. Then she came to the monster. "Are you serious?" she asked me. "Of course," I said. I was so happy.

We then went on a spending spree. I make a modest living, but to her, it seemed unmeasurable. I didn't mind. I loved her. New cell phones for her and her daughter. New cell phone for me too. We went to the casino way too much. I didn't mind at the time. I wanted to make her so happy. I didn't know that the train had no destination. We both agreed to marry at the county courthouse. In retrospect, an obvious question is, "Why so fast?" Well, the answer was pretty obvious. I'm not sure why, but I can tell you I needed someone to make legal decisions based on my health. Others had made suggestions, but the things they said were very upsetting to me. Maybe I should have listened. After all, the fact is far easier, isn't it?

Now we were legally married, but I wanted a ceremony where the Lord would join us. Marriage is not some contract that we sign between each other and whatever state we live in. We enter into a sacred agreement with the Lord as well. That would have to wait. At the time, my body was betraying me, and I was losing most func-tions, but at least I had someone who would love me through any-thing. She helped me in so many ways. Standing in the shower was difficult; she held me and watched me bathe. She dressed me, socks, underwear, everything. I found the most wonderful woman I could possibly comprehend. A week or so later, I was back home in New Jersey, and things were going south pretty quickly. My mind was being betrayed by the liver putting out poison. She called me during the day. I couldn't speak very well and felt incredibly tired. I told her I would like to take a nap and that she could call me later. She did. By then, I was in trouble. I could barely utter a word or comprehend what she was saying. She hung up and dialed 911 in Florida, which transferred her to North Carolina, which transferred her to New Jersey. An ambulance was on the way, I was told. I agreed, although I hate hospitals. But I knew I was close to a coma, and that meant being close to death. I put Shiloh in the backyard, so she wouldn't jump on the EMTs when they got there. I waited, in total confusion. They got me and went to put me in the ambulance. A woman asked me who the president was. I didn't know, I said. She told me it was Joe Biden. That's okay, I said, he probably didn't know me either. Pretty clever for a man losing his marbles.

They took me to a new hospital that had opened in our area and would not take me anywhere else. When I got there, the doctors took care of my stomach cavity and also drained the fluid surrounding my left lung. I began to feel much better very quickly. They put me in a room on a crowded section of the hospital. By now, I had realized that I did not bring my cell phone, and calling Florida friend would prove difficult while in the hospital. I was asleep when I felt my nose being swabbed. I did not authorize this, but the country had been consumed by fear of COVID-19, which I had already had. I had also been completely vaccinated. I had an IV, which I thought was normal, but it was causing itching. I did not get that right away. The next day, Florida friend was resting comfortably in my home only miles away. She had flown up quickly for me, which I thought was lovely of her to do. I saw the doctor maybe four hours later, and he told me I had COVID-19.

"No, I don't. I was vaccinated only three months earlier."

"You have antibodies," he said.

"Of course, I do. I was vaccinated only three months earlier, or did I just already say that?"

"Well, you are still confused."

So, is it that I have COVID-19, or because I am still confused that you are keeping me?" No answer. Oh well, I was feeling a lot better, and Florida friend would come get me, I was sure.

Another day went by and still chained to this bed. By now I had been scratching my arm so much I began to bleed.

"What is in this," I asked the nurse.

"It is to help you."

Didn't really answer my question now, did it? They were also giving me pills that either they didn't tell me, or I don't remember. Both were possible. Why haven't I heard from Florida friend? I was getting angry at this point. I spoke to the doctor again, and once again, he told me he would not release me since I had COVID-19. *I do not*, I thought. *The vaccinated do not get COVID-19!* I thought only the unvaccinated get it. He told me I still seemed confused and that he would not endanger anyone on the outside by releasing me. *I live alone! Who am I going to infect? By the way, you are standing right in front of me without a mask!* I insisted on leaving. Was told no, once again. *Where is my wife?* I started thinking of numbers and could not remember a single number from my phone, which was sitting at home. Ah! My mother's phone! I called; she said she would visit me. I told the nurses that I would be leaving when my mother got there. She would pass it on to the doctor, she said.

"Pass it on to whomever you choose, but I'm leaving. What is in this IV by the way?"

"Morphine," she said.

I instantly yanked it out. "I am trying to get on a liver transplant list, and you idiots are giving me opioids? I am not allowed to have them!" My arm was bleeding all over the place. The doctor came in once again and told me if I didn't calm down and do as they pleased, they would place two guards at my door and force me to stay! "Two?" I asked. I'm about 160 pounds and the weakest human on the planet and you need two? By the way, how do you think a combat veteran with PTSD will react to being threatened? My language and my behavior were unacceptable by then, and I was insulting everyone.

My mother got there and could not believe that the doctor would be so unprofessional as to force morphine on me without my knowledge. I was on my third day there, and Florida friend was nowhere to be found. I was furious. The doctor said once again that I was still cloudy. *No sh——t, dummy, you're giving me opioids! I'm stoned!* I called my Florida friend and asked if I had woken her up or if she was real busy watching *Little People, Big World* or something. She said no. I told her if she did not come get me out of this hellhole right then, it would be the shortest marriage in history. Not very nice, and since asked her for forgiveness many times. I just couldn't understand what this hospital was doing. She came and got me and lectured me on being rude to the staff. I agreed to work on it but had to ask why she did not call. She said she tried, but the hospital would not accept calls from a Florida phone number. That's why when I tried to call her, it did not work either. She also told me that she had been in touch with the doctor and that I was in good hands. *Didn't think to visit, though, huh? Three days? Nothing? Super fantastic,* I thought.

I later learned that hospitals get enormous amounts of money from the federal government (Pfizer) per every patient diagnosed with COVID-19. One large chunk of money for admittance and thousands per day they keep patience. That's lovely. I was held hostage by a hospital because they were broke and needed the money. No wonder the entire floor was filled. When we got back to my house, I had to inform the University of Pennsylvania about my opioid "use" and why. I was told I needed a blood test in three days, or I would be cast out of the program. I couldn't help but think that if I wasn't so rude and insistent to leave, they would have kept me for a week or more, and I would have been removed from consideration. Money can be evil, can it not?

At this point, I had sold my home in New Jersey. We were so broke financially until the check hit. It was $70,000. A very nice sum. We couldn't afford to go to Florida until the check hit. By this time, my disease had begun to diminish by mental capabilities. We went to closing on my house, and then my liver began to betray me even more. I could not concentrate. I could not think clearly. The thing about the liver is it takes care of everything. Whatever you eat or drink, your liver decides if it is healthy or unhealthy for your body. When you disrupt that, as I did, your liver begins to punish your body with toxins it normally would have removed. All of those toxins eventually go to your brain, so you can't think. I was learning what that was like. I was losing my cognitive ability. I could not remember who you were or what you intended. My brain was being hijacked by poison.

By now we were on our way and living in Florida. By this time, I bought a thirty-six-foot recreational vehicle that was beautiful. I also bought a truck to haul it. I was so proud of myself. I put down a total of $30,000 on these vehicles. We were going to seek and find my beautiful country. It did not come so easily. We bought the RV from Camping World in Port Richey, Florida. We were so excited to go on our first voyage. There was a problem, however, that nothing worked in the travel trailer we bought. The refrigerator was over-heating. We disconnected it. There were other minor problems that we overcame. But, on our first time, we had her drug addict brother and his wife along with us. I didn't mind, and I looked forward to it. We parked after a really difficult parking job. Nobody there knew how to park it. It was a wonderful time, I must say. I didn't mind the drugs my brother-in-law depends on, and we had a great time. I was still sick, but I loved the idea of spending months on the open road with my friend from Florida, even if she insisted her family come along. It was going to take some doing, learning the RV, but I was determined. Even if I could not lift a thing, I was determined. This is where I made a monster mistake. I could not give everyone the happiness they determined they deserved; at the moment they believe they deserved it. This was a critical error that I made, and I take full responsibility for it. We had a good time despite the growing pains of camping. We were in a great place. We were approaching do-or-die time. Either way, I really loved my Florida friend and her family. I was content.

One of my best friends during all of this, Todd, was visiting with his wife, Kim. Todd was bodybuilding at the time and was huge. It wasn't natural. We went out on the porch to chat.

Todd said, "I'm not into this God thing that you are. But I can see you are at peace."

I told him that he could have it too, in the next second. "Jesus has extended His hand. All you have to do is take it."

He said he was mad at God for what He was doing to me.

You have it completely backward, buddy. He is going to save me. If you blame God for all the bad things that life throws at us, who do you give credit to when things go well? Following Jesus is a simple decision, but a complex one too. Are you going to be one of those people who pray the plane doesn't go down and then get right back to sinning all over again when it recovers? If the building comes down around you, who will you cry out to? Through suffering we find salvation. I used to think of the apostle Paul all the time. He endured stoning, lashes, an actual thorn in his side, lost at sea, name it! Paul is involved in thirteen books in the Bible if I'm not mistaken. *That* is not a coincidence.

The Lord only asks for his belief through His Son. You cannot get to the Father otherwise. Simply believing is wonderful, but you must have an active relationship with the Lord. He has reached out His hand. If you take it, you take on responsibility and a much more fulfilled life. The Word says that we shall share this information with others in the hope that it will bring someone closer to God. I am still not fully convinced that I am one to do this. I know some of the Bible. I know some of His teachings. I am motivated by him every day of my life. Yet I am reluctant to save anyone else because of my limited knowledge of the Bible or its message. I told Todd, and I still do, that surrendering to a mighty power is not only logical but required. Do you believe that rain falls by chance? That our ecosystem is perfect? I've spoken about this. Do you really believe that all of this happened by chance and somehow you are here to say, "everything happens for a reason"? Whose reason? You already believe. Surrender to Jesus, and you will say it with pride.

Remember when I told you about the MELD score? Well, we were called to the University of Pennsylvania for a consult with the surgeon. At this point, my mind could not comprehend a conversation. The surgeon met with both of us, meaning the other person from Florida. When he spoke, I heard that I was putting my son in danger, when that was not what he said. He was telling me that I had a 10 percent chance of dying on the table. All I heard, however, was that my son was in danger. I stood up and said, "Thank you, but I am going home. My son will never be put in that much danger."

My friend from Florida grabbed me by the arm, and said, "No, you are in danger, not your son." I sat back down. I signed a bunch of things so I would not sue them for crap that would happen if I died. Hilarious. Fine, here you go. We drove back to Florida.

At this point, I was coming apart. Not only was I crippled by this debilitating disease but also the confusion that came along with it. At this point, I could not function at all. I would wake up in the middle of the night and pee all over. I would do the best I could not to fall down, as I didn't make it to the toilet. It was almost time, I guess. After a couple of days, we got another call from UPenn. Get back here now! Of course, I got the call but had to hand it off to my friend from Florida at the time to verify what I was hearing. It was verified. I asked point-blank, "Is my MELD score so dire as to demand my return at this moment?" No, I was told, just protocol. Yeah, right.

The next morning, my wife and I went to hook up our RV to our truck so we could save money from the months that I would require being there. We were given explicit orders to "hurry up," which indicated I would be dead soon. We went to the storage place that we chose, at 3:00 a.m. We had to get this hooked up and get our butts up to Philadelphia. For me. I know that I am oblivious here. At 3:00 a.m., my friend from Florida and I went to hook up the trailer. Others came to our aid when we failed, her brother and son-in-law. I should have been completely humble at this point, but I was not. I am now, for the hard work of these people. The problem was, we could not drag this trailer out of the Florida sand. We were stuck. I started to falter cognitively. I was losing reality. We needed to go. We jumped in my Ford Explorer and began the one thousand-mile trip back to the Northeast.

I was armed with the love that I was convinced was there from my Florida friend. I was safe; my Florida friend was going to take care of me. We crossed into Georgia, which wasn't that much of a stretch, considering it was three hours out of eighteen. We had stopped somewhere that I can't remember and stayed in a hotel. At this point, I was mentally gone. I soiled the entire room and acted out in a strange manner. My Florida friend decided maybe we should get out of here. We did. On the road through Georgia, my Florida friend asked me to drive, which I gladly approved. Why wouldn't I help?

After maybe forty minutes of driving, I realized that I kept driving off the road. My wife was sleeping, and I wanted so bad to contribute to the team by driving longer and letting her sleep. I couldn't, however, continue safely. I woke her and told her that I could not keep my course. My mind was almost completely gone at this point, by the poison that my damaged liver was feeding my bloodstream.

Not shortly after, my brain gave in to the onslaught of the poisonous things that made me almost crash. At this point, my body began to give out.

After only letting my friend sleep for thirty minutes, and her taking control, my body said, "Okay, I'm done." I was delirious, unable to function at all, let alone normally. And I soiled myself very badly. My Florida friend pulled into a rest stop that I believe said "Welcome to Virginia," but I cannot be certain. I do not remember much, but I do believe I loved, and still love, my Florida friend for caring for me at a time I could not for myself. My body and mind were almost useless. We went into the rest stop, and she stripped me bare of my soiled clothing and cared for me like a mother would her infant in the parking lot of Virginia. I am so proud that I knew my friend from Florida. This was absolute loyalty on display. I loved her for this.

We got to our hotel in New Jersey so we could be prepared what would be to come. I was still delirious, however, and that made for a difficult time for my friend from Florida. I was frustrated because I could not concentrate. I could not turn on the light to the bathroom and got very upset. She prayed that I would accept going to the VA to help my mental cognition. Of course, I said. We got in the car. She dropped me off. I was alone. This, of course, is not a big deal, but in my mind, I was being abandoned. After maybe forty-eight hours, my mind was returning to normal at least a little, but I was worried I hurt her. I cried for hours. I was also naked for some reason, without anything to cover me. My nurse kept coming in, and I was naked. This was a problem for me, but funny now for some strange reason.

We had been summoned to Philadelphia because I would be dead soon. Knowing this, we still had to wait fourteen days because of COVID-19. I thought, *This is crazy. I have to wait another fourteen days? COVID-19 or not, I'm going to be dead in days, not weeks.* All this time, I still worried about my son. He didn't deserve this, although I am completely proud of this man. He stepped up when there was nothing to think about. I was so unable to function physically, and the fact that my money from the sale of my home was dwindling, my Florida friend opened a GoFundMe account. I was completely uncomfortable with this, but I put her in charge. We were dealing with $1,000 per week in hotel costs, among others, and still have to pay all the bills at home. I had $17,000 in my account when we got there. We had to burn through so much just to have the opportunity to live. I was blown away.

I kept thinking, *What if someone was here without financial means? Do they just tell them to go home and die? What are the criteria that determine who lives and who dies? Come on, man. Seriously.*

When the GoFundMe account was set up, a friend I played football with in college contacted me. He asked, "What do you need?"

"To be closer," I said.

He arranged an Airbnb in Philadelphia. What a great friend. This was only six blocks from the hospital. Knowing my friend Greg, he bought something just to make our lives easier. The problem for me, however, was that row homes in Philadelphia were built maybe one hundred years ago. Therefore, one step is six inches, and the next is eighteen. I could not do the stairs. We stayed before surgery since I only had to worry about the steps once. I completely love the outpouring of support we got from everyone we have come to know and knew for a while. We were days from surgery now. I was counting the hours. I had never felt so much pain in my life; hope never again.

In the morning of the surgery, I was so upbeat it made others feel a bit put off. I was joking with so many health care professionals. My only problem was looking at the mother of my son, Brendan, who chose to save my life. I was wheeled in by my friend, and I saw my ex-wife. She was, in no way, happy with me. I was putting her son in danger. I felt guilty, of course. But it made me think of the groups that I have been in with the VA. So many guys tell others that they would be willing to die for their comrades and their kids. My response has always been "If you are willing to die for your kids, have the balls to live for them."

On this day, however, it wasn't about my duty or sacrifice; it was about my son's. My son was making that kind of commitment for me that morning. My Florida friend and I went back into the prep room. Nothing significant to report here; there wasn't much to it.

My friend and I talked for hours, waiting, and it reminded me how much I loved her and thanked the Lord that I had her. We talked and prayed for two hours, waiting for judgment day. We cried, we kissed, we prayed. I was completely ready to say, "Hey, Lord, I've done all I've come to do. Your call from now on."

When it was time to head into the operating room, the nurse gave us time to say our goodbyes. We had already done that, of course. I just wanted to say one thing. "If Jesus offers His hand, I have to take it."

My Florida friend said, "If He doesn't, I'll be here to take your hand." Wow, right? How can it get any better than this?

They had to take Brendan earlier, of course, because this innocent kid offered to save my wretched life. I was wheeled into the operating room. I was a bit surprised when I got there since only two guys were in there, and they did not seem of much importance. Then I began my stupid banter of teasing these guys, like "Hey, where is your scalpel?" "Dude, who's in charge of throwing out my terrible liver, and where does it go?" I was prepped for the doctors to come in. Then came the anesthesiologist, and I was still joking. He just said, "Hey, man, three deep breaths and then count to ten."

I wanted to impress them so much by being cavalier that I did as I was told and then counted to ten as fast as I could. Then I said, "Okay, so what I was saying is…" *Ha!*

"Two more times," he said. I did as I was told, and off I was. Do I wake or not?

I was out of surgery, and praise be to God, my son was safe. I can never understate the gratitude, shame in myself, but love for my son and the Lord. I did not deserve this. But I was determined to make this miracle of my heavenly Father a message for others. I'm not sure I am fulfilling that promise, but you can be the judge. Once I was out of surgery, I almost instantly felt better. I had been so used to feeling like garbage that it became second nature. I knew that the doctors said that I might be in the hospital for ten days, but I did not want to wait that long. I immediately looked and felt better. What are we waiting for? Friends from the entire world congratulated me for being a soldier in dealing with the horror of liver disease, and my sudden departure into, hopefully, a normal life. All the glory goes to the Heavenly Father. He gave my son to take on the role of saving my life. Brendan can never be thanked enough. I was so happy, but there was something that was bothering me. My Florida friend didn't seem very interested in my recovery.

After four days, it was obvious that my Florida friend had some kind of issue. She was staying in the Airbnb or whatever it's called that my friend Greg had arranged. It was a fine house, but there was nothing to do there. There was no cable. What could you possibly do while you were there other than sleep? Nothing. Still, she made excuses not to come visit me. I was very hurt by this. *There's nothing more to do where you are. I am sitting here, waiting to celebrate with you the life that we prayed to the Lord to save! He did. Why are you not interested anymore?* I was crushed and angry. I was on so many medications; many of them altered my emotions so that I did not behave all that well on many occasions. But still, Florida friend would call and say, "Maybe I'll be there at two." *What? What is it that is so important that you can't come see me at ten?* I handled this rejection poorly. On about three occasions, I let my disappointment be known to my Florida friend. I did it in a poorly constructed way. I was angry and hurt, and I let my emotions take over. Having said that, however, what wife would completely lose interest in a man who just fought for his life for over two years, win the battle, and *then* lose interest in him? This was unfathomable! Nobody can explain this. Nobody except our Lord.

Over the next several days, we had countless people come to see me and my wife. She was attentive and seemed interested. I could barely comprehend what was going on, being so doped up. I was proud, however, of my wife who would walk me through this. I was released, after badgering the doctors and working to gain strength by walking the halls incessantly. I needed strength to be released. The hospital and their staff were, and are, incredible. To take someone like me and care for me the way they did is almost hard to believe. Also, during my recovery, I saw my son. No way for me to express my love for him. It broke my heart every time I saw him in pain.

We were released to our gracious friend's Airbnb. I couldn't make the stairs, though, so it was worthless, unfortunately. My wife had to pack up everything we had, put it in my Explorer, and go somewhere else. I was very impressed with her determination because this was not an easy job. Once packed, we were back to the hotel at $1,000 per week. I have to tell you, finances were a concern, but mostly I was still very much in pain and just wanted to relax in a safe place. I had money left, but it wouldn't last long, hence the GoFundMe. I was embarrassed. At this point, I was very much new in the healing process and still had difficulty walking. I did it anyway. Every time I walked, so slow and with a purpose, I did it with a smile on my face to the other folks staying there and the staff. After a week, the staff would make comments at how I must be such a nice and positive man since I smiled all the time. "Of course, I do," I said. "I am lucky to be alive." My legs were so swollen with fluid they began to become a problem. I couldn't walk very well. In my soul, I wanted to shout from the rooftops that Jesus had saved me, yet I could not walk. I was in immense pain almost the entirety of the next six weeks. I could not sleep lying down. Each day that I praised the Lord, I also looked forward to the painkiller medication that was there to help me. Florida friend helped remind me that I did not want to exchange one addiction for another, but the pain was overwhelming.

The hotel was not so awful that I would complain much. It was a decent place, and I wanted to celebrate my recovery from this ugliness. I did not get the same message from Florida friend. She was frustrated at having to live in a hotel and have to attend to me far too much. Maybe I don't blame her. There were two incidents of me falling on my face that would have scared anyone. Florida friend had a lot on her plate. After maybe two weeks into my physical recovery, I began to urinate blood. It was not just a little; it was pure blood. It was 1:00 a.m. I told her that we had to go to the hospital, and within five minutes, we were on our way. We got to the University of Pennsylvania around 1:40 a.m. They checked me in. I peed in a bottle, had blood work, and waited to see if there was a major issue. One hour went by, then another, and another. After about five hours of sitting in some stupid room, I went out to the ER. There were maybe five of them laughing at some YouTube video. I was hot.

I asked one of them to inform whoever was in charge of them idiots laughing at a YouTube video that I was leaving. Florida friend objected in the strongest terms. The head of the ER also did. I said, "I've been here for six hours in the emergency room. Apparently, it's not an emergency to you, so it's not an emergency to me. I'm leaving." She told me that I could not do that. I got more hostile. "No? I came here voluntarily. Think you can hold me for maybe seven or eight hours? Look, I'm leaving." Florida got so upset that she began typing and calling her brother. I didn't much care at that point for anyone else's opinion. I wanted to leave, and I wanted loyalty from Florida friend. Instead, I got betrayed in a way I will never forget.

When I began to leave the ER, she had gone missing. While I was still in the room, she was gone. *Where? What the heck is going on?* At that point, I got an incredibly disgusting and insulting text message from her junkie brother, calling me of all things, a coward. I was livid. That word is the only word that I will 100 percent react negatively to, especially when you take into consideration that when I was serving my country overseas, he was serving time for being a dirt ball. I went down to the parking garage; there was my car. I went to get into the passenger's side and let Florida friend know how out of line she was to bring her brother into our marriage. I didn't know he was on speaker. He then took the opportunity to tell me, "Hey, go join the navy and get f——ked in the a—— again." I swelled with what can only be described as white rage. I saw pure white in my eyes. Not only did my wife betray our marriage by bringing some lowlife into our lives, but she also betrayed my trust for blurting out the one thing that ever happened to me that I kept to myself for over twenty-five years. This is a problem. Even typing this, I am a man of God, but I'm not sure I wouldn't take the opportunity to knock his last tooth out of his mouth. Lord, forgive me.

All this time, Florida and I have been looking for a house to live in. The housing market was still booming in 2021, and we were definitely going to overpay with whatever we determined we wanted. Back to suffering in the hotel room. Still couldn't sleep lying down.

Still in incredible pain. Through all this, she wanted a single-family home. We had swung and missed on two other occasions, having to pay inspectors and losing money. We were down a decent amount. I told her we should live in the trailer for a year and save money. That didn't go over very well since I got, "I ain't livin' in no trailer." Super.

Too much pride, I assume. Keep in mind, the trailer looks like a four-star hotel room. It was nicer than the hotel we were staying in at the time. To keep the peace, I looked at a house she had shown me and agreed that it was nice. I told her to call our realtor and have him go and take a look on our behalf. The resentment she had for me subsided, and she was back to being happy. Whew. That night, I was in an incredible amount of pain. Sitting in my chair trying to sleep, I was moaning or making too much noise. Florida friend whipped straight up in bed and yelled, "What are you moaning about?"

"Take a wild guess," I said. "I'm in a ton of pain!"

"Well, making all that noise isn't going to help!" she said.

"Oh, I'm sorry that my life-saving surgery and subsequent pain is interfering in your ten hours of beauty sleep." I wanted to say far worse, but I was pretty mad at that point. I knew this marriage wasn't going to work.

I vowed to try, and I promised the Lord I would do my best. My son, although with some difficulty, was making an incredible recovery, and that made me so happy. I kept thinking, *If I live and he doesn't?* Couldn't even imagine. We had done a tour of the home we liked via FaceTime with the realtor. Yes, let's take that one. By now, my finances had been crippled. But it was a VA loan, so we should be able to make this work.

BELLEVIEW

In January 2022, we moved in to a very nice home in a fifty-five-and-older community. My Florida friend got what she wanted. I was happy as well. We moved whatever we possibly could into the house. I was not much help as I was still very weak. But I did try to help out. The next day, she was talking to five neighbors, who huddled around her.

As I walked closer, one of them said, "Hear you just had a liver transplant!"

Wow, it didn't take her long to spread things around. I was a bit upset since people naturally make assumptions based on their previous experience or thinking. When I got closer, they mentioned that my Florida friend mentioned my surgery.

"I heard," I said to them.

One guy asked point blank, "What happened to your liver?"

"I drank myself to death. Next question." I had to laugh at that one. It actually made me laugh since the look on his face was that of shock.

Once we were in the house, my Florida friend started going bonkers about decorating it. I didn't mind, but at the same time, all my funds were at zero after the weeks spent in the hotel during recovery and closing costs. I made a fair living, and we had just blown through $70,000—a chunk of it by necessity. It was time to build back up.

Let me state right here that I cannot stand credit-card debt. I torment myself by the fact that they have the audacity to charge such high interest rates. I have made mistakes in the past about doing debt relief, which is a complete scam. It's like filing for bankruptcy, but you still owe the money back.

I did it once, my mistake. After making that mistake, my Florida friend educated me on the ins and outs of basic credit-card etiquette. Hard to believe that at my age, I did not know this. But the point is that I was working to get my credit rating back. Because of this miscue, it caused me to have my Florida friend be the actual buyer of the Ford F-150 that I put a large sum down on and the trailer as well.

Anyway, my Florida friend was doing a wonderful job making a home for the both of us, and I told her how proud I was. She really seemed to appreciate that. I was happy for the both of us. The house was beautiful, and I was on the mend, healing more each day. We had a wedding to think of in the next few months, and we were both excited about it. We were getting married at a borough hall so I could have someone in charge of my medical decisions. Looking back, that God she was given a decision, because she would have pulled the plug before the doctor finished his sentence about my condition. It would have been funny, looking back, if the doctor came out and said, "Mrs. Barratt, I just wanted to give you an update and ask you to make a decision."

She would have shouted out, "PULL THE PLUG!"

That—I would learn later, and so will you.

The house was wonderful, and I was so proud of her. We went to church each Sunday at a wonderful church in Ocala, Florida.

Meadowbrook Church has a wonderful pastor, Tim Gilligan. If you have not seen or heard of him, please search him on YouTube. He and his entire staff are wonderful. Please be kind in the fact that I just gave a plug to my church. I have to say, in the months that I have been a member of Meadowbrook Church, it has been extremely rare to find myself looking at my watch during a message by Pastor Gilligan. Before each service, there is music, like many other churches.

I was moved by the songs even if I didn't know them, and on many Sundays, I would find myself in tears. I went there the first time when I was very ill. I know the message that day was speaking to me. Once again, I felt the power of the Lord, and I heard there are no coincidences with the Lord. I wanted to be there. After surgery, when we started going there on a regular basis, I noticed an ad played on the monster screens they have. "If you sing or play an instrument, please see blah blah blah in the main lobby." I thought, *Jeez, what a wonderful opportunity to serve this church.*

My Florida friend and I went through their two-day instruction course of introducing ourselves to the church and us to them. We both went willingly and eagerly. I was now able to audition for the church choir and serve this church in any other way!

For the folks who have known me for years, writing these next few paragraphs is probably a waste of time because I doubt any of you will read them. So I'm safe. Just by some miracle one of these boneheads read this, I get a lot of questions about my faith.

Many have commented, "You have changed."

Yes, I have. I have seen the glory that comes with the power of the Lord. Do I say that? No, I don't. I simply offer that I find church to be a very positive place that offers me inspiration. Do you have a problem with positivity and inspiration? Thank you. Next question. Ha. They have come to accept my faith along with the realization that I am not perfect. I am a work in progress and will always be, God willing.

I signed up for an audition. I had been singing since I could speak, and to most who ever heard me speak, it was probable that they would prefer I sing.

"Shut up and sing," they'd say.

Anyway, I logged in to the church website. They had four songs listed but only asked that we record two of them and submit them to their website. Everyone who has ever heard me sing has said I have a wonderful voice. Hearing my own, however, is painful as I can pick out each flat or sharp part of my performance. When I hear myself singing, I don't mind it. But if I hear a recording of me singing, I cringe. I'm terrible. I recorded "Amazing Grace" and the other song probably twelve times. I saved them to my computer. Now for the upload and submission, uhh, try again. Huh?

File too large.

What? File was twenty seconds long? I can text larger than that! I tried again and again. Not going to happen. I emailed the person who sent me the invite and said to them, "Well, it must not be God's will that I do this because I simply cannot figure this out. Maybe next time." I offered. I got an email later telling me that (I'm paraphrasing, not what they actually said) yes, we have other complete idiots that can't figure out this simple task just like you, so we will gladly forfeit personal time with family for your completely stupid self. Okay, of course, that's not what they said.

I spent hours trying to remember the lyrics of the songs that they sent. They sent four, but all I had to do was commit two to memory. *I can do this.* I played these songs over and over for days. I watched them on YouTube and Rumble over and over. Okay, the songs were a bit high for me, but I could pull it off.

I am a second tenor, which means nothing to most people. Okay, let me put it this way. I am not Steve Perry of Journey. In fact, no one is. That is completely off-the-charts first tenor. I am not Barry White either, the soft-toned person who could say good morning, and it would sound magical. I am in the middle.

*****

I knocked on the door to let me in so I can blow this audition and move on with my life. I met with a woman who ran the moment-to-moment. I was given two songs that I had to sing, and wait a minute…*these two songs?* I memorized the other two songs! It was not going well. Now I had dry mouth, was sweating, and flat-out embarrassed. The whole entourage of feelings went through me. There were only about seven of us there—only seven twits who couldn't figure out how to upload, whatever. Now I was in a bind. They assured me that they would make accommodations for me. However, I felt like screaming! My time came. I walked on to the stage and was given a microphone. First, I had never been, one bit, intimidated by performing in front of strangers, not once. I had driven a golf ball with others watching. I had briefed high-ranking officers to defend my country. What did I have to fear if I knew what I was saying? The problem came in the form of me not knowing the songs they intended for me to sing! They changed their order for me. I felt so low then. But when the music played, I sang the way I always have. Clear, on tune. Man, wow, I blew that out. I sounded great.

I'd never felt that way before. I remember walking off the stage and a lady accompanied me and mentioned that I never seemed nervous at all.

"What do I have to be nervous about?" I replied. "I sing either on stage or thirty feet away in a seat way over there." My point is, if I am singing, I am singing for the Father, not some crowd. The Lord is my crowd. I joined the choir shortly thereafter. Amen, right?

*****

We were living strong in our faith and going to church every Sunday, as expected. I remember when the pastor went over Ephesians 5:23–25. These passages mention a man and woman in marriage. The man shall love his wife, as the Lord had His church, which he died for. Yes, I am in. Ephesians 5:25, the wife shall honor her husband as the head of the household. Of course, I am paraphrasing. But when I shared that with her in church, she recoiled and laughed at it as the pastor was talking about the importance of marriage. No, this was not going well. She claimed to be a woman of God yet determined what and when she would believe in the Bible and our Lord. I gave my heart not only to her but to the Lord that blessed our home. She was cherry-picking what she would adhere to and what she would reject. This was not good.

We enjoyed our company and headed out to lunch after church. I was growing more and more healthy as time went on. We were looking forward to our upcoming official marriage and had much to plan for. I noticed, however, that she began to show signs of disinterest in me. No interest in what I said, did, or where I went. The one thing she did was read my emails, track my every movement, and stalk me, basically. She had done this once or twice before while I had just been given a new life, months earlier. I had never dealt with jealousy before. But this was much more nefarious and sinister. Something was not right. I didn't get it. I was soon going to swear to the Almighty God that I plan on being with you alone for the rest of time. She searched my emails, snuck around, and checked me out. This was weird. I let it go. I wanted to keep the peace. Who had hurt this woman so much that she felt obligated and entitled to follow my cell phone and send got-you texts? I just shook my head and powered on.

We had done the best we could with the resources we had to plan a wedding that we could both appreciate. I hired a cook that would serve fillet and a wonderful menu. I hired a DJ so we would have music. She was in charge of the actual presentation of the wedding. We hired a wedding planner as we both wanted nothing but the best for our special day. Of course, we could not afford the $6,500 bill. We both took out loans via credit cards. We both understood that we were in this together. The day came; however, in early April, there was a major storm coming. Now I was in a bind. I wanted what my soon-to-be wife wanted, and I would do whatever to get her what she wanted.

"The only thing I can't control, honey, is the f——ing weather!"

She told me over and over that the Lord would not violate our day and to have them set up in the backyard as planned.

"Jeez, woman, can't you see the weather reports? Babe, I want you to have the best day of your life, but I can't control the weather!"

She had me set up in the backyard. The skies opened up, as if the Lord did not approve, or so I think now.

I was in a difficult position. My soon-to-be wife wanted what she wanted. Weather didn't care, and she tried to defy it. Now what? I was so bogged down with a horrible feeling that someone called to tell her she was blowing this. Amen, at least it wasn't me that said it. As I said, we live in a fifty-five-and-older community. We got the clubhouse to do it. I never felt so lucky marrying this lady who did the unthinkable when I was sick and dying. I apologize for this, but she bathed me and wiped me. How much loyalty can you have? Thick and thin? Good times and bad? Charge forward, please, and realize that you found the best thing that ever happened to you, right? I had my pastor from home, Jeff, minister our wedding. I was making a holy vow not only to my Florida friend but to the Lord Himself. I cried most of the ceremony or tried to hide it.

Jeff never approved of the union with my Florida friend. I was warned repeatedly not just by him but by others as well. However, I wanted what I wanted. Our wedding was incredible, and of course, I sang "Tangled Up in You" by the band Staind. Oh boy, did I love this woman! Also sang "Word of God Speak" by Mercy Me, which was my favorite, and I sang it proudly. I sang two other songs but had to include my son, who saved my life. It was a perfect night. But my liver was making other plans.

I started itching again a week prior. The other bodily functions seemed off. Then I ate pesto by accident, which I find revolting. I had to retire for the cleanup that needed to happen since we did this in our old-people hall or whatever you call it. I couldn't do it. I vomited over and over. My son and his love both were there as well as my baby, Kelsey. Did you really think I wanted to foul this night up by being sick? Loved our time together with our families, but now what? Flights were canceled because of overbooking (airlines, you are awful) and traffic. High school "spring break" was going down. Never even heard of such a thing, but I had my head in the bowl giving up a $50 fillet. Don't mind me.

COLLAPSE AND SALVATION

When the dust cleared, look, something wasn't right. At first, I gave everything a pass. After paying off all her bills for life, I realized that with the things she bought in our home, I was running out of resources to pay for all of it. My anxiety level was going a bit higher. On top of this, please forgive me for bringing up the fact that now I was much healthier, I was willing to be intimate. However, it was not happening. Hmm, what's up with that? Why, after all this time, would she not reach for my hand at night in an intimate way? She had no interest in intimacy. Wow. I had a hard time with that. Our engagements were short and get-off-me type of things. I didn't like it. Why would any man accept a relationship under God and have half of that union balk at sharing intimacy? On the other hand, it was difficult for me to perform as it were. Yes, please take that in and carry on smartly. When we tried to be intimate, I could tell she had no interest. This was so sad to me. She never once asked me about anything. She was not interested at all. Even when she would commit to being intimate, the fact that I could tell she had no interest made it too difficult for me.

Okay, now we were roommates. Wonderful. Well, if we were nothing but roommates, we should share in the responsibility of paying the bills and stop hanging all this stuff around the house.

She spent so much money for trinkets around the house that I was losing it in the sense of where is the money coming from now? I was growing increasingly frustrated. "Stop spending, let's spend time in loving each other!" She had no interest. We had the travel trailer that "we" bought, and I wanted to spend time with her while learning how the heck to actually camp! Our first trip was interesting, but it was before my surgery, and it was over and done with. So I will leave her family out of this—shaking-my-head stuff. We, in total, used the RV four times. Each time, she didn't want it for me and her to go together. There always had to be someone else. Well, she had arranged our honeymoon to be in Georgia. I was looking forward to it because she was simply with me; however, it blew up in my face. We really did enjoy our time together for a while; we played board games and laughed together at each other. I was really happy. The weather opened up with tornado-type stuff, so we had to cut our honeymoon short. I was happy though as I had her to myself. But later, I had to hear that our honeymoon was my fault and not the weather. I kept praying.

We made it through some horrific storms that battered many, without harm. It was April, after surgery in November 2021, and we still had not consummated the marriage. I kept thinking, *Why is she with me at all?* Sex is not everything, granted, but this was weird. Take into account that she had been snooping in my emails after a short time, stalking me on the phone application, and then not having any interest in intimacy? I was already confused and was growing bitter. She had not married me for healthy reasons. There was something wrong with our relationship. Of course, as I tend to do, I blamed myself for not making enough money, for not looking good enough for her to desire. What could I do?

The Amazon deliveryman came every day. I would ask, "What now?" I would get "It's 'only' X amount." Yeah, every day of this delivery can't be sustained. I was growing worried that the only reason this Florida friend married me was so I could fund some bizarre lifestyle that I didn't understand. The bills, which I had paid down to zero, began to climb again. At first, it wasn't a big deal. I had to take out a loan myself to fund the wedding she wanted. I had no idea of the extent of the damage and never asked. I wanted nothing more than to keep the peace.

When intimacy went out of the picture, I looked for what I was here for. I wanted a partner whom I could share our lives, decisions, everything with. She had no interest in it. Now I was growing resentful. I was being used for my finances. This really seems incredible since my income was modest, but compared to someone who made

$12 per hour for fifty years, I guess her expectations changed when she met a man four months from death with a government pension. She hit the jackpot.

"I can marry this guy, spend four months with him, watch him die, and live better than ever before."

Yeah, I am sorry to say, that not only is this some crazy theory, but it is true. I have been conned, people, by a con artist who would have loved nothing more than to see that I choke on my own vomit to end my life, for when I am gone, she could claim survivor benefits for life. After all, she earned it, right? She worked for six months helping me. Look, turn your head when I say that I paid her a total of over $10,000 just to help me.

"Six months, so I can watch this man die."

Terrible. I know. I wish it were not true. I prayed harder and harder, but unfortunately, I began drinking again because the anxiety was back at very powerful levels. Yes, you read that right. I drank again. Unbelievable.

She married two other men that caused her harm in some way; she was now entitled to whatever this dying moron owns. "Who cares, just die already. I have spending to do, and a guy that is clinging to life."

You know, this was difficult for me to type. I am a kind man. I have limitations that I am aware of, and I try every day to improve. But the one thing I cannot stand is disloyalty. If I make a mistake, tell me about it; we can make it better. As the months wore on, I asked about her spending. She still held the secret. I was also paying for her daughter's phone even though she was thirty-three years old and working. Her husband hadn't worked for years or contributed to the family, something I was new to.

"How can you not work? You are young, able bodied, so work!"

Nope, not for years when I met him and not since. They kept him out of work to improve the chances of food-stamp checks coming. Probably not isolated to this one couple, but I found this vile. The young man can work for his children but chooses not to because someone can pay him to not work. The point is, this is the kind of person I married. She was always looking to scam the system, "Get *me* some that I owed!"

Owed for what? Being an American? Waking up in the morning? Look, go raise your right hand, and after a few tours, come on back. We'll talk. But regarding this deadbeat stay-at-home father? Hard to imagine what I got myself into. I believe in personal merits; they believe in "who can we scam?" today. I got completely wound up in this, to my eternal regret. Unfortunately, I married a person with the same goals. I am so sorry to type this, I have been scammed. I gave my heart to this woman. She gave me nothing but had many demands. As a result, I began falling apart again. Resentment built up in me, and I went for couple of drinks that I should not have. I needed the Lord now more than ever.

I was singing in the choir as I could. I enjoyed it and still do. I would sit there in church and imagine all the folks that were so much less off than I was and thank the Lord for the air in my lungs. Great stuff. At this point in our relationship, I realized that it was nothing more than a financial transformation that needed to happen. I was, by then, helping with her finances that I had no idea about. I knew she spent around the house as I did. I had $1,000 in debt from the wedding. I was aware of some of her accounts and offered to help. I had no clue that she, in six months, had run up her credit-card debt to almost $20,000. How is that even possible? How can you possibly spend that much money in only six months? I learned later that she had run up old accounts in her last husband's name and blah blah blah. Oh boy, I began paying many of her bills; it didn't matter.

I began drinking a little during our time of stress—once here, once there. Nobody noticed. I did, of course, but still. I mentioned it to her on one occasion that I had three drinks. She confidently said to me, "Don't do it anymore." It wasn't an order. She offered it as support. Loved her for that. The more I realized that I was being used as a credit card, the more resentful I became. Drank a few more times, mostly when she was in bed. If we were just roommates and I paid *every bill*, why should I hide it? She should be paying most of her own bills and thank me every day that she has the ability to live here at all! I had a poor disposition that was not getting any better.

I was so resentful that I pray our heavenly Father may forgive me. I drank approximately seven times in six months, but she started taunting me. She was looking for a fight, something I just wanted to downplay and move on with the night.

"Yes, I have been drinking but please go to bed. Don't worry, I'll pay your bills in the morning so you can live on with your dream of never paying a bill you accrued ever again in your life." I missed the mark, however. What she wanted was a free ride from some sucker dude as a result of all the wrongs life had given her. I had been tested so many times by people with nefarious intentions; it absolutely destroyed me that I had one here. The good news is, it happened quickly, I guess.

Painful to type. Awful behavior by me and her. I snapped at her on two occasions when I knew I was being used for my money. Not proud of it. I got took, people. Plain and simple. This woman married me strictly so I would die and she could have what I don't regard as that much money to herself for life. Now I knew I was a target by someone with dark intentions. Here it was again—the darkness that seems to always challenge me—my inability to back down. I was in a difficult situation. I thought she love me; she loved what I could give her. I was completely distraught. With this information, I drank more. The evil voice over my right shoulder was in the midst of winning again. I couldn't take it.

We were struggling to get along, and I was uneasy. I didn't know how to handle what was going on. I thought if I married a godly woman, nothing could make us go off the rails.

One day, I decided to play poker, which I had done on maybe six occasions while we were together that I did not share with her. I had a conversation with Todd about his situation one morning and was aggravated. I had been continually tracked by someone who was not interested in me. She went through my emails, checked my phone, given me grief for months about giving to those less fortunate without my permission. I was in a boiling-point situation. She mentioned where I was as a "gotcha" moment. I blew up. I went and opened an account in my name only and drove home. I went crazy on her about respecting her man and all that ego garbage that comes along with it. She called me a coward during an argument, which did not fly with me. I did not handle it well. I made her afraid of me by shaking my fist.

She was having stomach discomfort at the time. So that was my first priority. It had gotten so painful that I was concerned for her well-being. I dialed 911 since I could not lift her off the bed and help her because of her size. The EMTs got there and took her to the emergency room. I grabbed her things and followed. Before I went in, I noticed that she had been demoralizing me in text messages to her friends. She was setting the tone to divorce me and shake me down for money. I didn't concern myself with that at the time since I had been praying to our Lord for her health. She had diverticulitis, an inflammation of the lower intestine. Praise Jesus, she was going to be fine. I cried so hard she had to tell me to stop. About two hours after we got her home, the doctor called and said she had chlamydia. I was shocked when she called to me out of the bedroom what it was. I told her. She had a sexually transmitted disease. I made no judgment initially; I had to comprehend what I just heard. She sprung out of bed despite her intense pain and blamed me within five seconds of me telling her what it was.

"You must have given it to me!"

"Uh-huh, don't think so."

I got tested the next day at the VA and was clear of any infection at all. Hmm, she had been unfaithful. What to do with this knowledge?

Not only did I expect, as the Bible does, that she leans on me as the head of the household (Ephesians 5:25), but to show appreciation for all that we both had at the time. I waited for contrition and an admission that she had strayed. Maybe embarrassment, humility? None of that happened.

Later, she would say to me, "I haven't done anything wrong. I am not a sinner."

Wow, a perfect person. I thought only Jesus was perfect in human form. Not only did she not show any kind of contrition or humility, she went on the attack instead. I was shocked. A woman of God was telling me all this was my fault, that she did nothing wrong. I asked her for over a year to cut her daughter loose and let her pay her own bills. My requests were ignored. I asked for over a year to stop tracking my every movement, to stop stalking me! I was there simply to pay for her life, not to share it with me. Now there was proof of infidelity.

I drank one night. My head was spinning at what to do about this situation of marrying a woman who said she was a woman of God yet turned away from the very things that God demanded. These were not my demands; they were directives from our heavenly Father! Had she even once shown me a bit of humility—I am not typing this right now. She had absolute disdain for me at this point, having gained knowledge in destroying men's lives in the past. She had a plan for me, AND SHE TOLD ME HERSELF! I have voice messages telling me that she had a plan to remove me from my own home.

I am so ashamed to have been involved in such a story of God's love and human frailty. My failures jump at me daily. I beg forgiveness from our heavenly Father. At this point, however, how do I handle a woman living with me who betrayed me *and* blamed me for her own actions? I woke up the next morning. I turned her cell phone and her daughter's cell off. I got sick of paying for the phones they actually used to condemn me every night. She taunted me for not being a man for over an hour. I begged her to go to work and leave me alone. She refused. She knew how to get me upset. She pummeled me with insults as I grew angrier and angrier. At one point, I slapped a cup out of her hand. The sheer look of joy on her face was evident, and it was the pure face of evil that I had ever seen. She was so lucky in her mind. She dialed 911 and claimed she was so afraid of me. She would not leave, for some reason, for someone so afraid. But I was placed under arrest for striking her.

Charges were completely ludicrous, of course, and not true. She knew that the moment she touched the phone. I was forced out from my home for over ten weeks while she sold almost everything she could get her hands on. She had robbed me of my joy in living in God's name. She had soiled our vows to the Lord after getting married, which my very good friend, Pastor Jeff, officiated. She had spit in the face of the Lord while she claimed she serves Him. All those warnings from friends about money. All the messages that I disagreed with. All the warnings from the dark side of things that make suggestions over my right shoulder. I was more of a target now, as a man of God, than ever. I was targeted by darkness in the form of a godly woman. That blew me away; I never saw it coming.

I have said enough of my Florida friend at this point. She feels entitled and owed, like her kids who don't and will not work. I have been covered in shame for having fallen for it.

The beautiful part of this is that I am back in my church, Meadowbrook in Ocala, Florida, back to my choir, which will start again soon, and back to speaking to people that regard human beings as meaningful! I am also working on my master's degree in marriage and family therapy focusing on trauma in an effort to help other veterans with PTSD. This is a very exciting time in my life. I am still a spiritual target, it seems. If I look back over the last two years, I have to pause and thank the Lord in heaven.

I began as a lost person. I was completely distorted about what life was supposed to be. I was lost. Then disease took me over, and my will was tested. I had no choice; I could not give up despite the pain and sorrow. When I hit my knees, it was the most incredible moment of my life being completely surrounded by nothing but love—only the love that Jesus can provide. I have met the prince of darkness *and* the one and true Lord and Savior of our lives. I have been tested more than most. I fought through bad behavior and bad decisions. I was given a choice and a chance. I was given a hand that reached for me. I took it.

The one and true God of my life makes all possible despite my distractions. I have to tell you; after heading off to uncertainty at the hands of only a man with a scalpel, there is no way, under the sun, that there is such thing as a coincidence. They do not exist. It is the Lord's will whether you believe it or not. I would like to share a message of hope despite the darkness that continues to follow me.

Believe.

To me, believing is knowing. When people ask how I know, I ask them if they love their spouse or brother-in-arms. They always answer in the affirmative. How do you know? Can you define what it feels like to love? Think about it. Define what love is. Reach for Jesus. He has been there all along. He knew you before a drop of water was in the ocean. He knew your name, what you would do, who you would be the moment He intentionally laid on that cross for you!

I come from a military background. We don't leave a man behind. Try comprehending a man, yes, a man, being tortured and dying for all of us, even the ones who deny Him. That, to me, it is something I can never live up to. The good news is, He does not ask me to.

There was a time after my baptism that I was having the same dream for eight or nine nights. It was the devil himself whispering in my ear that the Lord did not love me, that I could not withstand the challenge of my disease. I was told to give up. I remember telling the devil that I am clothed in an impenetrable white armor of the Lord. I asked my pastor about it.

"We will always be targets of darkness," he said. "We are beyond the grasp of the devil, and he does not like that."

I scanned the Bible, and of course, I found Ephesians 6:11, which says, "Put on the whole armor of God, that you may be able to stand against the wiles of the devil." It was fitting that Paul shared yet another message with me. No coincidences.

There was a scene in *The Chosen* where Little James, a man with limited physical abilities, was asked to spread the Word of the gospel with the authority of God to heal. James was unnerved. He did not understand his role in this since he had a physical challenge. Jesus asked if he would like to be healed, and of course, James said he would like that very much. Jesus then explained to him how much more vital it would be to have a man with a physical limitation to spread His word while healing others. It was incredibly powerful and made me think of all the days I was weak with no hope and all the days when I was angry and resentful. I had felt hate in my heart but tried to remember that hate only erodes the one who carries it. I had been incredibly blessed.

There is much this writing of mine can share to those who give it time to read. Reading, if understood and given careful consideration, can be powerful. Hearing without listening can waste any man's time. I have no agenda or expectation of this. Only that I love the Lord more each day. I have been troubled at times; I get it. But I think of all that has been gained by the suffering and terrible mistakes I made over time! I was told by my dear friend that I had peace. Even in my darkest hour, I had peace. My response to him is the same response I give to you. You can have it too, and you can have it this second. Take His hand, my friends, take it now.

May you find inspiration. May you find justice for those seeking it. May you find peace in the name of the Father. And if you mourn those you have loved, I can't resist to quote Abraham Lincoln, "May our heavenly father assuage the anguish of your bereavement and leave you only the cherished memory of the loved and lost."

God love all of you.

> Blessed is the one who perseveres under trial because, having stood the test, that person will receive the crown of life that the Lord has promised to those who love him. (James 1:12)

Shiloh

Kelsey HS Graduation

Illness Catching Up

One month post transplant

Shiloh in Fall

10 days after surg

Baptism 2021

Closing Ron

Jeff and Buck

Liver disease

Ron sick

Brendan, who donated his liver to save my life.

About the Author

Ronald Barratt is a disabled veteran of the United States Navy. During his life, he has had many dark moments. In his first published book, *Sailing Into Salvation*, Ronald describes those dark times that were followed by amazing miracles of faith and healing. In the eighteen months of a fatal illness, Ronald was determined to live. He realized, after surrendering to our Lord, that the power of healing was in the hands of his Creator. This is a story of his travels through incredible pain and suffering to the miracle of the Lord's grace. It is his hope that the reader will find inspiration in the story contained here.

Ronald Barratt is a graduate of the College of New Jersey. He joined the US Navy in 1992 as an intelligence analyst. Ronald has two children, Brendan, who helped the Lord to save his life, and Kelsey. Ronald was determined to survive his horrific ordeal to show the world that Jesus Christ always has his hand out, reaching for us to take his hand. It is Ronald's intention to inspire, never give up hope, and most importantly, realize the depths of God's love. We can do all things through Christ who gives us strength.